The Financial T
Investment Trusts

PEARSON

At Pearson, we believe in learning – all kinds of learning for all kinds of people. Whether it's at home, in the classroom or in the workplace, learning is the key to improving our life chances.

That's why we're working with leading authors to bring you the latest thinking and best practices, so you can get better at the things that are important to you. You can learn on the page or on the move, and with content that's always crafted to help you understand quickly and apply what you've learned.

If you want to upgrade your personal skills or accelerate your career, become a more effective leader or more powerful communicator, discover new opportunities or simply find more inspiration, we can help you make progress in your work and life.

Pearson is the world's leading learning company. Our portfolio includes the Financial Times and our education business, Pearson International.

Every day our work helps learning flourish, and wherever learning flourishes, so do people.

To learn more, please visit us at **www.pearson.com/uk**

The Financial Times

With a worldwide network of highly respected journalists, *The Financial Times* provides global business news, insightful opinion and expert analysis of business, finance and politics. With over 500 journalists reporting from 50 countries worldwide, our in-depth coverage of international news is objectively reported and analysed from an independent, global perspective.

To find out more, visit **www.ft.com/pearsonoffer/**

The Financial Times Guide to Investment Trusts

Unlocking the City's best kept secret

John Baron

Harlow, England • London • New York • Boston • San Francisco • Toronto • Sydney • Auckland • Singapore • Hong Kong
Tokyo • Seoul • Taipei • New Delhi • Cape Town • São Paulo • Mexico City • Madrid • Amsterdam • Munich • Paris • Milan

PEARSON EDUCATION LIMITED
Edinburgh Gate
Harlow CM20 2JE
United Kingdom
Tel: +44 (0)1279 623623
Web: www.pearson.com/uk

First edition published 2013 (print and electronic)

© John Baron 2013 (print and electronic)

The right of John Baron to be identified as author of this work has been asserted
by him in accordance with the Copyright, Designs and Patents Act 1988.

Pearson Education is not responsible for the content of third-party internet sites.

ISBN: 978-1-292-00156-2 (print)
      978-1-292-00510-2 (PDF)
      978-1-292-00509-6 (ePub)
      978-1-292-00797-4 (eText)

British Library Cataloguing-in-Publication Data
A catalogue record for the print edition is available from the British Library

Library of Congress Cataloging-in-Publication Data
Baron, John, 1959-
  The Financial times guide to investment trusts / John Baron.
    pages cm
Includes bibliographical references and index.
  ISBN 978-1-292-00156-2 (pbk.)
  1. Mutual funds. 2. Investments. I. Financial times (London, England) II. Title.
HG4530.B335 2013
332.63'27--dc23
                              2013022344

10 9 8 7 6 5 4 3 2
17 16 15 14 13

Cover image © Getty Images

Print edition typeset in ITC Stone Serif 9.5/14 by 3
Print edition printed and bound in Great Britain by Henry Ling Limited, at the Dorset Press,
Dorchester, DT1 1HD

NOTE THAT ANY PAGE CROSS REFERENCES REFER TO THE PRINT EDITION

To Thalia, Poppy and Leone,
with my love
And to those who have helped me,
with my thanks

Contents

About the author

John Baron is best known to readers of the FT's *Investors Chronicle* magazine for having successfully run two live investment trust portfolios as measured by their appropriate APCIMS Growth and Income benchmarks. His popular monthly column explaining portfolio changes is closely followed. It aims to help investors – private and professional – with their investments.

John has used investment trusts in both a private and professional capacity for over 30 years. Upon leaving the Army, he entered the City as a fund manager running a range of portfolios for private clients and charities. He was a Director of Henderson Private Clients, and then a Director of Rothschild Asset Management having been approached to run its private client core UK equity portfolio.

Upon entering politics, John has sat on the other side of the fence helping charities monitor their fund managers. He remains a member of the Chartered Institute for Securities & Management.

His message is that investment is best kept simple to succeed. Complexity adds cost, risks confusion and usually hinders performance. This philosophy runs through this short but revealing book about the City's best-kept secret.

Acknowledgements

We are grateful to the following for permission to reproduce copyright material:

Figure 2.1 from Moore, E. (2012), 'It's an open and closed case for fund investors', *The Financial Times*, 25–26 February © The Financial Times Limited. All rights reserved; Figure 2.2 from Walters, L. (2011), 'Fund performance tables hide bad records', *Investors Chronicle*, 19–25 August, using data from Lipper; Figure 5.2 from Barnes, D. (2011), 'Synthetic appeal', *Securities and Investment Review*, October; Figure 5.3 from Ross, A. (2011), 'Understanding ETF risks, investors warned', *The Financial Times*, 24–25 September © The Financial Times Limited. All rights reserved; Figure 8.1 from *Securities and Investment Review*, August 2012.

Table 2.1 from Walters, L. (2012), 'Investment trusts beat open-ended peers', *Investors Chronicle*, 27 July–2 August, using data from Lipper, Morningstar and Canaccord Genuity Wealth Limited; Table 2.2 from Walters, L. (2011), 'Trusts that beat their mirror funds', *Investors Chronicle*, 1–7 April, using data from Canaccord Genuity Wealth and Morningstar; Table 2.3 from Walters, L. (2011), 'Investment trust fees on the rise', *Investors Chronicle*, 3–9 June, using data from the Association of Investment Companies (AIC); Table 2.4 from O'Neill, M. (2012), 'Performance fees in decline', *Investors Chronicle*, 14–20 September, using data from Lipper; Table 3.1 from St. George, R. (2012), 'When the price isn't right', *What Investment*; Table 4.3 from *What Investment*, March 2013; Table 7.1 from Duncan, E. (2012), 'Act now', *What Investment*, May; Table 8.1 from Clarke, G. (2011), 'Multi-manager funds serve up few benefits', *The Financial Times*, 19–20 November © The Financial Times Limited. All rights reserved.

Text on pages 124–6 from Baron, J. (2013), 'Japan: a once in a lifetime opportunity?', *Investors Chronicle*, February.

In some instances we have been unable to trace the owners of copyright material, and we would appreciate any information that would enable us to do so.

Foreword

Investment trusts have been the City's best-kept secret. They perform better and are cheaper than the unit trusts and open-ended investment companies (OEICs) that dominate the nation's investment and savings market. Yet many private investors, charities and smaller pension funds are simply unaware of them.

This is going to change. The introduction of the Retail Distribution Review at the beginning of 2013, and other changes to financial regulation, will be one catalyst. Others will include far greater awareness of investment trusts' many advantages. The secret is about to be let out of the bag and investment trusts are about to have their day in the sun.

Investors need to be ready to benefit. *The Financial Times Guide to Investment Trusts* will help you better understand investment trusts. Characteristics such as their structure, gearing and discounts will all be explained as will other factors that affect how trusts perform and are perceived. I will also discuss the stepping stones to successful investing, and how to construct and monitor a trust portfolio. Finally, I will explain the workings of the two live and benchmarked portfolios that I have been sharing with *Investors Chronicle* magazine readers in recent years.

As any investor will know, knowledge is the bedrock of successful investing. This book aims to explain the potential of investment trusts in a clear, concise and jargon-free manner. It shows their apparent complexity is a myth – a myth which has tended to obscure investment trusts' merits to professional and private investors alike for too long. I hope readers will then see the wonderful opportunities on offer.

Happy investing!

Introduction: The changing landscape of investing

Why is it so little is known about investment trusts? After all, they have been around for a very long time – many trace their ancestry back to the nineteenth century. Some of them are very large with market capitalisations of around £2,000 million – not easy to miss! Sections of the financial press often talk about the merits of investment trusts, including better performance and cheaper fees when compared with the unit trusts that dominate the market. And yet, the typical investor is unaware of them – the first chapter will therefore explain what investment trusts are.

Most of us love a bargain. So why have we been over-paying for our investments? Why is it that, in the past 10 years alone, the amount invested in unit trusts and open-ended investment companies (OEICs) has risen three-fold to over £600 billion, whilst assets held by investment trusts have only grown less than 50 per cent to around £100 billion? And why is it few investors outside the wealth managers in the City know about them?

The answers are various. But the common thread linking them is a competitive landscape which has been tilted against investment trusts for some time. All this is about to change.

The key catalyst has been new regulations that came into force at the beginning of 2013. Hitherto, many investors have turned to an independent financial adviser (IFA) to help them run their portfolios. Most of these professionals have earned their money not by charging the client a fee, but rather by receiving commission payments from the managers of the products they sell to the client.

Investment trusts do not pay commission to IFAs. Open-ended funds such as unit trusts do. As a result, there has been an in-built bias in favour of these open-ended funds, which is why they tend to dominate the retail market.

Some clients might have thought they were getting 'free' advice as they could not see fees coming out of their pockets. Most clients would have been aware of the arrangement but perhaps hazy about the scale of commission fees paid to their IFAs. Whichever, there is no free lunch. The commission fee has been deducted from the product sold, and therefore comes out of a client's overall investment returns.

In the UK, much of this changed in January 2013 when new rules were introduced by the Financial Services Authority (FSA) as a result of the Retail Distribution Review (RDR). These rules now ban commissions. Instead, IFAs are now expected to earn their fees by charging the client directly themselves and up front. The fee may be an hourly charge depending on the time spent or a fixed fee depending on the type of advice. Whichever, the effect will be the same – fees will be paid directly by the client.

One aim of the RDR is to make charges much more transparent. The theory is that clients will now more readily understand the fee structure. Another objective is to eliminate potential conflict of interest claims against IFAs – regardless of how well they have served their clients in the past. Meanwhile, the FSA has ruled that the new adviser-charging structure should not commercially disadvantage clients when compared with the old commission fee arrangement. Time will tell whether the RDR has been a success.

But whether a success or not, the RDR's effect on investment trusts will be profound. These trusts can now compete with the open-ended funds on a more level playing field. No longer will they have an in-built disadvantage when being recommended. The gloves are off and the fight is on. And investors are set to benefit as a result.

However, this is only half the story. The advent of the RDR is certainly a catalyst for change, but investment trusts have been the poor cousin to the more dominant unit trusts and OEICs for a number of other reasons – although this too may be changing.

In the past, investment trusts have not always been good at setting out their stall. They are a slightly more complex beast when compared with the open-ended funds that have dominated most clients' portfolios. But this complexity has been grossly exaggerated, possibly by those with vested interests.

Yet where were the marketing campaigns to sell the product? Compare this omission to the massive marketing by the unit trust and OEIC managers, especially each year when the new ISA season approaches. Where could investors get a simple explanation of how investment trusts work? Certainly not from the banks or building societies.

And, perhaps more importantly, where have investors been able to find those advisers willing and able to use investment trusts to their clients' advantage? The major exception has been the private client wealth management operations. Typically, these have served their clients well, but they have traditionally been the preserve of charities and private investors with £500,000 or more to invest.

This failure to reach out to investors has not been helped by the odd bit of bad publicity. Some investors will remember the 'split-capital' investment trust scandal. During the late 1990s, these trusts were marketed as low-risk investments, particularly for those seeking income. But it turned out they had borrowed from each other in what was dubbed the 'magic circle'. High gearing and intricate cross-holdings made for a volatile mix. The detail is unimportant, but a number of investors lost out after the market crashed in early 2000.

Though severe for those involved, the bad publicity was out of all proportion to the scale of the affair. Only a few fund managers were felled by the scandal, but it threw a dark shadow over most of the investment trust industry. The episode seemed to confirm for many that investment trusts were a dark art best avoided, the characteristics of which bordered on mysticism. It certainly did not help the industry's profile or appeal to investors.

However, this perception is slowly changing. There has been more coverage in the financial press highlighting the better performance of investment trusts compared to their open-ended cousins, and often by some margin. The press has also confirmed that investment trusts are a cheaper way of gaining exposure to markets – an issue of increasing importance. These two facts are not unrelated.

And more investors are coming to appreciate their other useful features. These include the ability to 'store' dividends and so produce a growing stream of income for investors even when markets are rocky – helpful for long-term planning. Increasing awareness that their structure is better suited to certain asset classes, such as private equity and infrastructure, has also helped.

In short, investment trusts are beginning to combat the ignorance and sometimes prejudice that has characterised attitudes. The momentum is slowly moving in their direction. However, there is one further factor in this changing landscape. The RDR and better awareness of trusts' advantages apart, there has been another force bubbling away – which may now be coming to the boil.

There is a growing realisation – in part driven by ageing demographics and poor finances – that the country's population needs to do more financially to prepare for later life. The pressure is on government finances, and this will not change for decades to come. The penny has dropped and various government initiatives abound. One example is the subtle yet significant changes to the inflation indexing of state pensions. The government's latest attempt to encourage more people to take up a pension is another. More effort to teach basic finance to school students is yet another.

In addition, people are finding it harder to access debt – the financial 'system' is less sympathetic and this is likely to continue for some time. The banks have tightened up lending to businesses and individuals alike whilst continuing to repair their balance sheets and mitigate against future risk. Interest rates on credit cards remain stubbornly high despite interest rates in general being close to zero.

Furthermore, the financial climate is less sympathetic in another sense – less tangible, but important all the same. Today's generation does not have the same trust as previous generations in its perception of certain assets. Yesterday, there was an almost unshakeable belief that house prices would go up over the longer term, pensions were safe and worthwhile, and that the stock market would rise. Banks were considered trustworthy. Not today. Instead, there is greater uncertainty and, with it, a view that more self-help is necessary.

This view has been reinforced of late by news that many high street banks are exiting the financial advice market for customers with less than £100,000 to invest. Further evidence of a potentially large 'advice gap' has come from a recent survey quoted in the *Investors Chronicle* which found that two-thirds of financial advisers said it would not be profitable to advise clients with less than £50,000 to invest.[1] It is these very people who need good financial advice more than much wealthier clients. In addition, a *Financial Times* survey[2] suggested that one-third of those with more than £50,000 in liquid assets would now stop using IFAs when charged directly under the RDR rules. More and more people are now contemplating DIY investing – whether through necessity or choice.

Given these various factors in this changing landscape, making your money work harder and greater awareness of the range of investment possibilities on offer becomes more important. There are many people for whom this information will become more relevant. And in the search for more cost-effective and better returns, investment trusts will be one of the key beneficiaries.

For too long investment trusts have remained the City's best-kept secret. Their moment is approaching when they will step out of the shadows and into the glare of investors – both large and small. The challenge for the industry is to explain clearly how they work and how they can serve investors.

I hope *The Financial Times Guide to Investment Trusts* will play a small part in achieving this goal. Chapter 1 explains what trusts are and how they differ from unit trusts and OEICs. Chapters 2 to 4 will cover the pros and cons of trusts including performance, fees and discounts. Chapter 5 looks at some other factors which will further help investors make informed investment decisions.

The following three chapters (Chapters 6 to 8) then focus on how to construct and successfully run a portfolio. They cover the importance of mapping out your investment objectives, the secrets of successful investing and several other tips and pointers. Finally, Chapter 9 talks you through my Investors Chronicle portfolios as a way of illustrating the key themes of this book.

Investors will be well rewarded if the opportunities and risks of investment trusts are better understood – very well rewarded indeed!

1

What are investment trusts?

Investment trusts do have a slightly more complex structure than unit trusts or open-ended investment companies (OEICs), but therein lies the opportunity for those investors who take the time to understand them. The effort can be very rewarding!

Structure and differences

Most investors will have at least some element of their portfolios invested in funds. The concept is simple. An investor will join many other investors in pooling their money and, in effect, giving it to a fund manager to invest. Such an approach is sensible – it means investors can access a diversified portfolio and so lower risk, whilst the costs are lower because they have been shared.

Most funds are unit trust or OEICs – both being 'open-ended'. These are so called because when any investor buys or sells them, they are directly adding or subtracting from the pot of money invested in that fund and managed by the manager. In doing so, as investors buy and sell, they are creating or cancelling shares in line with investor demand.

Open-ended funds

Before purchase		**After purchase**
Fund size = £1,000,000	Investor buys 10,000 units @ £1 each	Fund size = £1,010,000
1,000,000 shares in issue. Therefore each share = £1		1,010,000 shares in issue. Therefore each share = £1

But there are other funds called investment trusts. These are listed or public companies and as such are 'closed-ended' in that they have a fixed number of shares: they are 'closed' after the initial launch or share issue. Their shares are listed and traded on the stock exchange like other public companies such as Shell, Marks & Spencer and GlaxoSmithKline.

Instead of specialising in the management of oil, clothes or drugs, investment trusts specialise in the management of portfolios – typically of other quoted companies. Their purpose is to make profitable investments in financial assets for the benefit of their shareholders.

By buying the shares in Shell, M&S or GSK, an investor is not adding more oil, clothes or drugs for the company to manage. That is for their managements to decide. Likewise, buying the shares of an investment trust does not add to the size of the portfolio. You are simply buying part ownership of the company itself – not adding to the underlying portfolio – in the hope of profiting from its successful management.

Closed-ended funds

Before purchase		After purchase
Portfolio size = £1,000,000	Investor buys 10,000 shares through the stock market	Portfolio remains £1,000,000
1,000,000 shares in issue. Share price reflects demand and supply in the stock market		Shares in issue remain 1,000,000. Share price continues to reflect demand and supply in the stock market

If Shell, M&S and GSK manage and grow their assets well and profits increase as a result then, all things being equal, this will be reflected in a rising share price – to the benefit of those shareholders who own the shares. Whether these companies succeed will depend on a number of factors, such as the economic environment, the business model and above all the quality of management.

Similarly, investment trusts strive to grow the value of their portfolio of stocks. Success or failure will eventually be reflected in the share price of the trust. Factors such as the economy, the method of research and stock selection, and the investment acumen of the manager will all play their part.

But essentially, the business of an investment trust is the same as that for any other quoted company – to make money for those who hold its shares by growing assets under management.

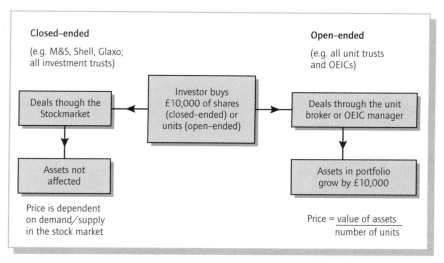

Closed-ended

(e.g. M&S, Shell, Glaxo; all investment trusts)

Open-ended

(e.g. all unit trusts and OEICs)

Investor buys £10,000 of shares (closed–ended) or units (open–ended)

Deals though the Stockmarket

Deals through the unit broker or OEIC manager

Assets not affected

Assets in portfolio grow by £10,000

Price is dependent on demand/supply in the stock market

Price = value of assets / number of units

Figure 1.1   Open-ended v. closed-ended trusts

Net asset value (NAV)

In the case of investment trusts, the assets are the portfolio values and a common way of pricing this value is by referring to the net asset value (NAV), which is the value of the portfolio divided by the number of shares in issue.

By way of example, let us assume that today the total value of ABC investment trust's portfolio of stocks, shares and cash is £100 million. There are 100 million shares of ABC in issue. The NAV is therefore £1.00 (£100 million value divided by 100 million shares). If, in the future, the value of the underlying portfolio was to rise to £120 million because the stock market and therefore the portfolio had risen, then the NAV would rise to £1.20 (£120 million value divided by 100m shares), and so on.

The NAV is a useful way of relating the value of the portfolio to the share price, and is closely watched by investors.

Discounts and premiums

Being closed-ended with a fixed number of shares, the share price of an investment trust is not dictated by the underlying value of the assets under management – the NAV – but rather by the extent to which investors wish to own the shares of the trust itself. Trading in the shares does not affect the value of the NAV.

As such, the share price can be more or less than the NAV. If it is less, the trust is said to be *trading at a discount* (see Figure 1.2). Most investment trusts trade at a discount to NAV. Presently, discounts average between 5–10 per cent. This effectively means that an investor is buying £1's worth of assets for 90–95p.

This reflects that, historically, institutions have been sellers. It may also reflect the fact that investment trust prices can be a little more volatile than those of open-ended funds. This is because their price is not only affected by movements in their NAV (like open-ended funds) but also by movements in the discount (unlike open-ended funds). Investors may therefore be seeking compensation or a margin of comfort for holding investment trust shares.

A discount to NAV is not necessarily an opportunity. A large discount may, for example, also reflect low confidence in the fund manager – perhaps because of poor performance – or a dislike of the trust's focus on a particular region or sector. It can also reflect the fact the investment trust is not communicating well its investment strategy to the market – investors do not like uncertainty.

If the share price is more than the NAV of the underlying portfolio, then the trust is said to *trade at a premium*. There may be a good reason – the fund manager may be well respected, or the underlying focus of the portfolio very much in fashion. But beware, as buyers you are effectively paying an additional charge for obtaining exposure.

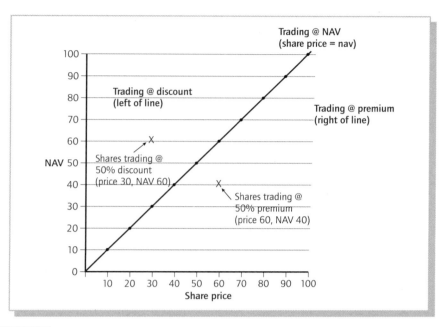

Figure 1.2   NAV and share price

This ability of share prices to trade at discounts or premiums to NAV can present wonderful opportunities and risks for investors. This is something covered in later chapters, but for the moment it is important to recognise that this characteristic of discounts and premiums does not exist with unit trusts and OEICs.

Price and size

Being public companies, the price of investment trusts is decided by how keen investors are to own the shares – there only being a limited number. The price will rise if there are more buyers than sellers, and vice versa.

By comparison, being 'open-ended', there is no limit as to how many shares – or units – can be created by unit trusts or OEICs if the demand exists. Prices are dictated directly by the value of the underlying portfolio and not by investor demand. The individual unit price is decided by the value of the fund divided by the number of units in existence, and not by the extent to which investors want to own the shares.

Being public companies, the size of investment trusts in terms of market capitalisation is therefore decided by the number of shares in issue multiplied by the price of those shares. Murray International Trust has 118.9 million shares in issue which means a share price of £10 equates to a market cap of £1,189 million. By comparison, the size of unit trusts and OEICs is decided by how much money investors have placed in that particular fund – as reflected by the number of units in existence.

Investment trusts vary in size enormously. The largest have a market capitalisation of around £2,000 million, whilst some of the smallest come in under £10 million. The larger tend to invest across markets globally and access all the major markets. These are typically suitable for investors with smaller portfolios who may just want to start with a few investment trusts. The smaller trusts tend to have more specialist briefs such as smaller companies, equity income or bonds.

Range and reach

All public companies invest in and manage a portfolio of assets. Like other listed companies, investment trusts tend to specialise in certain categories of assets. Just as Shell specialises in oil and M&S in clothes and food, different trusts will manage different assets – be they equities, property, bonds, private equity, etc.

Whatever the asset, the fund manager's objective will be the same: to buy and sell the portfolio's assets in the hope of outperforming the benchmarks for the benefit of shareholders.

Being 400 in number, investment trusts offer a huge range of investment opportunities covering all global markets and a diverse variety of asset classes. The investor is spoilt for choice.

For those just starting and who may only want to hold a few, there are the large generalists such as Scottish Mortgage, Alliance and Foreign & Colonial. These can roam the global markets and make decisions on your behalf as to which investments are best. If cautious about the outlook, they can take defensive action such as raising cash levels and bond exposure, but their brief is essentially to invest in equities (the shares of other public companies) for the longer term.

For the more experienced investor and those whose assets allow them to have a spread of trust holdings, then the world is your oyster! Investors can create a portfolio of trusts to reflect their risk tolerances, income demands and market outlook. There are investment trusts to suit every taste. From the UK market, one can choose a combination of growth, income growth, high income, medium-sized and smaller companies.

Looking abroad, all the markets are covered – from trusts covering continents to individual countries. These include 'emerging' markets and 'frontier' markets, such as the remote parts of Africa. One can also combine themes. For example, if income is important but you also want overseas exposure then the two can be combined. There are trusts offering exposure to Latin American, European and Far Eastern companies with decent dividends – to name just a few.

Furthermore, there are trusts that focus on all sorts of specialist or thematic areas – bonds, commodities, infrastructure, life sciences and technology for example. Globalisation does mean that there are many profitable themes to be pursued that transcend national boundaries. And investment trusts have the full coverage. Indeed, some have access to areas that closed-ended funds simply cannot access or replicate – one being RIT Investment Trust, which is the personal investment vehicle of Lord Rothschild.

A comprehensive (but not exhaustive) list of categories under which most investment trusts operate is as follows:

Global – growth	Global – specialist
Global – income growth	Global – smaller company
UK – growth	UK – income growth
UK – high income	UK – high income/smaller companies
UK – mid cap	UK – small cap
UK – fledgling	Europe – general
Europe – smaller company	Europe – high income
US – general	North America – income
US – smaller company	Japan – general
Japan – smaller company	Asia Pacific – ex Japan
Asia Pacific – including Japan	Asia Pacific – income
Asia Pacific – smaller company	Asia Pacific – single country

Emerging markets – global   Emerging markets – income
Emerging Europe   Latin America
Emerging markets – single country

And:

Bonds	Commodity	Financials
Environmental	Alternative energy	Infrastructure
Life sciences	Technology	Timber
Utilities	Private equity	Property
Hedge funds		

The following chapters cover the many advantages of investment trusts over their open-ended cousins.

2

Better performance and cheaper fees

It is a little known fact that investment trusts have not only performed better than unit trusts or their benchmarks, but have also beaten their 'mirror' funds – their unit trust equivalents run by the same trust manager. The key, but not the only, reason for this is cheaper fees.

Better performance

With open-ended funds dominating the retail market, you would have been forgiven for thinking that unit trusts and open-ended investment companies (OEICs) were the best collective investment vehicles in town. But you would have been wrong. History shows that investment trusts have soundly beaten the performance of their open-ended cousins over the longer term.

As you can see from Figure 2.1, financial advisory group Collins Stewart compared the performance of investment trusts to both unit trusts/ OEICs and their relevant benchmarks (local stock markets) over the 10 years to 31 December 2011. The results were revealing.

Investment trusts have produced better returns than their benchmark indices – local stock markets – in seven of the nine regional sectors analysed. In addition, they have outperformed unit trusts in eight of the nine regional sectors. Japan was the exception, largely due to the

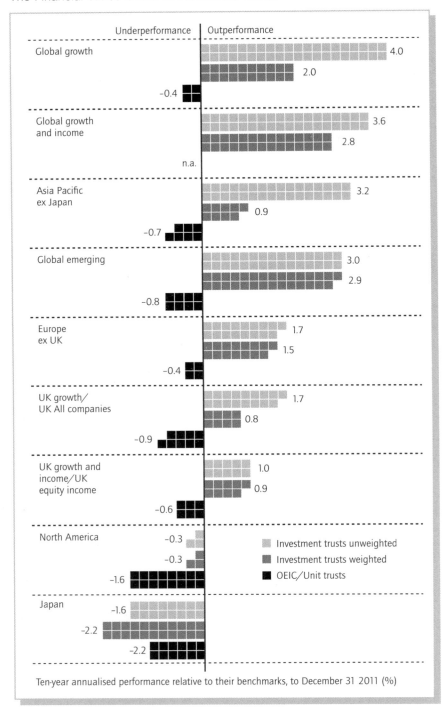

Figure 2.1   Investment trusts v. unit trusts v. benchmarks

lacklustre performance of the largest investment trust in the sector, JPMorgan Japanese. Performance differentials were greatest in the global growth sector where trusts' NAV growth averaged 4.4 per cent a year, compared to just 2.4 per cent from open-ended funds.

Perhaps just as damning for unit trusts and OEICs is the fact that, over the same period, not only did they come second to investment trusts in all but one sector, but they also underperformed their benchmarks in every sector analysed. The same is true of one- and five-year figures.

You could argue that I am being unfair to open-ended funds! Why? Because the performance figures cited above relate to the share price of investment trusts – and not their NAV. Remember from Chapter 1 that, being a closed-ended fund, investment trusts have issued shares like other public companies to be traded on the London Stock Exchange and abroad. As such, the price of these shares can rise and fall according to investor demand.

This means the shares often do trade at a different value to the assets held in the portfolio, and discounts can and often exist – the discount arising when the share price falls below the value of the underlying portfolio (or NAV). And, over the past decade, average discounts have narrowed from around 11 per cent to 8 per cent: in other words, the share price has risen faster than the NAV by about 3 per cent. This has boosted the returns of those holding the shares, and flattered the share price performance of the investment trust relative to its underlying portfolio or NAV.

In order to show that investment trusts really have performed better, we need to look at how successful they have been at growing their NAVs – and not just their share prices – and compare this to unit trusts and OEICs. Otherwise, you could accuse me of cheating! There is only one value for unit trusts, whereas investment trusts have two – their share price and their NAV.

It is therefore useful to look at Table 2.1. This focuses on comparing the NAV performance of investment trusts and unit trusts/OEICs over a 10-year period to 31 May 2012.

The table confirms that, in most cases, investment trusts' assets or NAV have beaten both the relevant benchmarks and the NAV of unit trusts and OEICs. It also confirms the pedestrian performance record of the open-ended funds relative to the benchmark. Canaccord Genuity calculates that the annualised outperformance over both open-ended funds and relevant benchmarks in the core regional sectors is 1.93 per cent and 1.35 per cent respectively.

Table 2.1   Ten-year asset performance to 31 May 2012

	Investment trusts	OEIC/unit trusts	Benchmark
Global	174.1	140.2	148.4
Global equity income	187.3	na	148.4
UK equity income	165.2	146.8	144.1
UK	178.3	150.0	158.1
North America	139.1	122.6	142.6
Europe ex UK	173.2	143.4	147.2
Global emerging markets	398.9	298.7	325.6
Asia Pacific ex Japan	286.7	247.1	282.2

Source: From Walters, L. (2012), 'Investment trusts beat open-ended peers', *Investors Chronicle*, 27 July–2 August.

The figures also bring into stark relief the extent to which these annualised outperformance figures add up over the years. The figures quoted above may not sound large but it is too easy to forget what a powerful cumulative effect this outperformance can have on a portfolio, particularly over 10 years. Investing £10,000 in the Global sector in an average investment trust would have produced an NAV of £17,410, compared with £14,020 for open-ended funds – a significant difference.

These are of course average figures. Many good unit trusts and OEICs do beat their benchmarks and the poorer performing investment trusts. But having a better performance average increases the chances of profitable investing for investors: it is easier to reach your objective if the current is with you.

It is also true that there are some sectors where comparison is not possible. In the fixed-income sector, for example, there are few investment trusts compared to unit trusts or OEICs, and so no meaningful comparison can be achieved.

However, the charts and figures tell a convincing story: investment trusts have outperformed open-ended funds over the past 10 years, over most meaningful timescales, and in almost all of the major comparable sectors, whether you're comparing share prices or NAV. The same is true when comparing investment trusts with their benchmarks. Rarely in the investment world is the evidence so conclusive – it's an open and closed case!

Beware unit trust tables

I also want to reinforce the message that, in many cases, past performance tables flatter unit trusts and OEICs. Performance figures do not always indicate past performance because there have been many fund closures, predominantly in the open-ended sector, resulting in poor track records being removed from the equation. The assets of a poorly performing fund are then added to a better-performing fund whose performance figures are then quoted going forward, or are added to a new fund launch, or are simply returned to investors.

Either way, the poor performance figures are hidden from view. Fund management groups spend a lot of money marketing their products in what is a very lucrative industry. The last thing they want is the media and investors being able to highlight poor performance figures that could tarnish their record and the record of their better performing funds. The stakes are too high. Better to remove the poor figures entirely, and focus attention on the good news.

This is more of a common occurrence than many investors would imagine. Figures from the Investment Management Association (IMA), the fund industry's trade body, reveal that the investment fund industry undertook a near 100 per cent turnover of funds between 1998 and 2010. Nearly one fund was closed or merged and another launched for every working day over the period. The total number of funds launched in those 12 years was 2,660, while there were 2,486 'closures' including mergers. This is a phenomenal turnover rate, given that the total number of funds in existence at the end of 1999 was 2,437 – little changed from the 2,574 at the end of 2010 (see Figure 2.2).

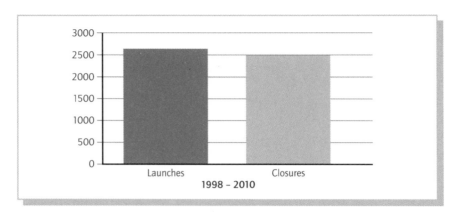

Figure 2.2   Fund launches v. closures, 1998–2010

Source: From Walters, L. (2011), 'Fund performance tables hide bad records', *Investors Chronicle*, 19–25 August.

This is why many clients have questioned why the performance of their unit trust holdings has never been as good as the tables would indicate – their poor performance no longer exists! Indeed, it could be argued that five-year sector-average performance statistics reveal only half the story – the good half. Certainly 10-year data should be taken with a pinch of salt because of the near total turnover in funds and therefore performance.

A further disadvantage of unit trusts is the expense involved. The closing and then merging with or launching of other funds, on the scale highlighted above, is costing millions of pounds in consultancy, tax and legal fees. And guess who is paying?

The strange case of 'mirror funds'

Could the better performance of investment trusts be explained because trusts have employed better managers with different investment goals and strategies? Different football teams have different managers who produce different results, even though they are playing in the same league. It would be a logical explanation.

However, this is not the case. Many fund management groups have the same managers running both open- and closed-ended funds. It makes commercial sense. All the technology, systems and people are in place so there is little duplication of effort or expense. And with open-ended funds charging higher fees, it can be a lucrative business.

Further research by Collins Stewart confirms this is not the reason. It has compared the performance of investment trusts and unit trusts that have the same fund manager and similar, if not the same, investment strategies and goals. Over 20 comparisons were made and Collins Stewart found that more than three-quarters of investment trusts performed better than their open-ended equivalents, despite having the same fund manager in charge. Table 2.2 highlights some of the comparisons.

The outperformance figures are annualised and we have seen previously how this adds up over the years on a cumulative basis. But the real message here, in many cases, is the difference in performance. Logically, this should not be happening. Why should the same fund manager with the same investment brief and benchmarks produce such different results? What are the factors contributing to this?

The answers to these questions go to the very heart of why investment trusts perform better than their open-ended equivalents.

The effect of cheaper fees on performance

The media has been understandably obsessed with bankers' bonuses. But there is another area of the financial sector that deserves similar scrutiny yet largely escapes attention, much less admonishment – unit trust management charges.

When comparing the performances of both funds run by the same fund manager, it is interesting to note that the unit trust charges are significantly higher. On 15 April 2012, *The Sunday Times* compared the performance of two funds run by Neil Woodford – the Invesco Perpetual High Income Fund and Edinburgh Investment Trust. Over three years, the unit trust had returned 58 per cent having charged an annual management fee of 1.5 per cent. The investment trust had returned 100 per cent, yet had charged only 0.7 per cent.

The same is true of other fund managers. Harry Nimmo runs both a unit and investment trust called Standard Life UK Smaller Companies. The unit trust returned 111 per cent having charged 1.6 per cent, whilst the investment trust returned 152 per cent having charged a more lowly 0.8 per cent management fee.

Table 2.2 Investment trusts that beat their open-ended equivalents

Investment trust	Total expense ratio (%)	Discount/premium to NAV (%)	Outperformance of equivalent (%)*[1]	Open-end equivalent fund	TER(%)[2]
Aberdeen Asian Smaller Cos	1.57	−4.66	0.7	Aberdeen Global Asian Smaller Cos	2.04
Aberdeen New Dawn	1.21	−7.83	1.8	Aberdeen Asia Pacific	1.84
Baring Emerging Europe	1.23	−10.18	1.6	Baring Eastern European	2.0
BlackRock World Mining	1.47	−14.43	2.7	BGF World Mining	2.07**
Edinburgh Dragon	1.29	−8.19	2.0	Aberdeen Asia Pacific	1.84
Fidelity European Values	0.94	−16.18	1.8	Fidelity European Fund	1.68
Fidelity Special Values	1.24	−9.60	1.3	Fidelity Special Situations	1.69
Henderson Far East Income	1.26	2.82	3.7	Henderson Asian Dividend income	1.56
Henderson TR Pacific	0.92	−10.50	1.4	Henderson Asia Pacific Capital Growth	1.77
JPMorgan European Smaller Cos	1.21**	18.27**	5.6	JPMorgan Europe Smaller Cos Fund	1.68**
JPMorgan Emerging Markets	1.21	−7.84	1.2	JPMorgan Emerging Markets Fund	1.67**
Jupiter European Opportunities	1.17	−6.67	1.6	Jupiter European Fund	1.79**
Lowland	0.73	−6.57	1.7	Henderson UK Equity Income	1.75
Polar Capital Technology	1.19	−0.94	0.1	Polar Capital Technology Fund	2.76**
Ruffer Investment Company	1.22	6.44	2.7	CF Ruffer Total Return	1.54
Temple Bar	0.57	−0.70	0.7	Investec UK special Situations	1.61
Templeton Emerging Markets	1.28	−6.28	7.0	Templeton Emerging Markets Fund	2.5**

1 Net asset value total return annualised.

2 TER supplied by provider unless otherwise indicated.

Source: From Walters, L. (2011), 'Trusts that beat their mirror funds', *Investors Chronicle*, 1–7 April.

Is it a coincidence that the better-performing investment trusts charge significantly lower fees? I suggest not. But higher charges by open-ended funds are not restricted to such 'mirror fund' situations. Unit trusts generally charge higher fees – typically 1.5 per cent, but they can be higher. Higher fees can only be taken from one source, the fund's underlying portfolio, which in turn reduces its performance.

In trying to quantify the effect of higher fees on performance, we should start by looking at the effect of fees in general. They make a big difference to returns over the longer term, particularly if one is starting with a lump-sum investment.

Assume a client invests £11,280 in a self-select individual savings account (ISA), and it is left for 30 years earning 6 per cent a year – a not untypical return. With no charges, except for a small capped fee to the provider for administration, it would be worth £61,940 at the end of the term. A management fee of 1.5 per cent a year brings the value of the same portfolio down to just £41,169 – a whopping one-third less.

Various statistics are available to help clients quantify the difference higher fees can make to their returns. One of my favourites assumes a client invests £100 a month for 30 years in both an investment trust and a unit trust. We are told that both funds grow by 5 per cent a year, and that the management fees are 0.75 per cent for the investment trust and 1.5 per cent for the unit trust. Not a big difference you might think. But after 30 years, the investment trust will have returned £71,800 compared to £63,100 for the unit trust – a significant difference.

However, although the above investment returns and charges are based on evidence, the examples are academic exercises. The fund management firm TCF examined the returns of the three main fund categories recognised by the IMA – 'active', 'balanced managed' and 'cautious' – according to total expense ratio (TER, see later). It analysed how both the cheapest 25 per cent and the most expensive 25 per cent of funds compared with the average performance of funds in each category over three and five years.

The results were revealing. In both the 'active' and 'balanced' categories, the cheaper funds performed on average 1 per cent better per year than the more expensive. In the 'cautious' category, the cheaper funds outperformed by around 0.6 per cent a year – producing an average performance of 2.9 per cent a year compared to 2.3 per cent for the more expensive.

Now these figures may not sound like big differences, but by now you will recognise that small figures become large ones over the longer term. If an investor could increase the performance of £10,000 invested over 25 years by 1 per cent a year – from 5.5 per cent to 6.5 per cent – then the increase in the total sum at the end would be more than the original sum invested. It is worth thinking about. The unit trust industry thrives – intentionally or not – on investors' ignorance about the extent to which time transforms small numbers into bigger ones. Do not be caught out!

A small but growing number of unit trust managers are recognising that such high charges are indefensible. A few, for example, have launched hybrid funds that combine low fees and active fund management in return for a cut of any outperformance over the benchmark. However, these are few and far between. Despite tentative signs that the penny has dropped, the majority of the unit trust industry still over-charges when it comes to fees.

You could legitimately argue that it is worth paying for good performance, and you would usually be right. But we know that unit trusts tend to underperform both investment trusts and their benchmarks. Most unit trust fund managers fail to beat their benchmarks and higher fees are one of the main reasons.

Indeed, costs are a key indicator of future returns. Every pound of management cost is a pound taken off performance. Expense ratios need to be much more closely monitored by investors and advisers alike – choose funds or trusts with lower costs, unless consistently good performance warrants paying more.

Lesson from America

To illustrate the point further, we should look overseas. Figures from US mutual funds (unit trusts) seem to confirm that low-cost products usually outperform high-cost ones. Having adjusted for the fact that US funds tend to be cheaper because they are larger in size, the average

TER (fees and costs combined) is around 0.9 per cent. This compares to around 1.6 per cent for our unit trusts.

Again, it does not sound much but it has helped US managers to consistently outperform their UK rivals. Research by Lipper in 2011, commissioned by the *Financial Times*,[1] showed American global equity funds having returned 32 per cent more than their equivalent British unit trusts during the past 15 years. The research pointed out that, in the past decade, US funds beat UK funds across every sector including Europe. The reason put forward was the difference in fees.

Other research focusing on the US confirms the message. When looking at the period between 2005 and 2010, Morningstar found that the cheapest US equity funds returned on average 3.35 per cent a year, compared to just over 2 per cent for the most expensive. In fact, over any time period tested Morningstar found low-cost funds beat high-cost funds every time.

Be careful of hidden charges

When investigating further as to why American funds are cheaper, you cannot help but conclude that it is the differing fee structures for financial advice. As we know, in Britain independent financial advisers (IFAs) used to receive a commission from the open-ended funds they sold the client. So these funds had to charge an extra fee – typically 0.5 per cent – to cover it. Whereas in the US, advisers charge clients directly for their services, and so there is no need for commission charges to be added to fund costs to compensate. Such is the thinking behind the Financial Services Authority's Retail Distribution Review (RDR).

The message is simple. Although the difference between 0.75 per cent and 1.5 per cent on an annual basis seems small, over the longer term this difference can have a huge effect on portfolio returns. And this is one of the key reasons – if not the key reason – why the same fund manager adhering to the same brief can produce such different returns when running an investment trust and unit trust.

It is strange that in this more transparent world – assisted by the internet – where customers increasingly buy goods at a discount to asking price, that investors do not ask more searching questions about fees when considering investment decisions. And these decisions usually involve relatively large sums of money. The fact that fund charges in the UK are almost twice as high as they are in the US can no longer be ignored.

The TER and more

In order to help investors when asking searching questions regarding charges, I cover the current debate about fees – both declared and hidden. We have established that higher fees significantly erode port-folio returns, so it is important to check the costs of investing.

The total expense ratio (TER) is considered a better measure of overall costs given that it does not just include the annual management fee but also other costs such as administration, legal and audit fees, together with any performance fees levied by the fund manager. This TER is then presented as an annualised figure.

For those wondering, the good news is that the TER of investment trusts remains significantly cheaper than that of open-ended funds. Research from Lipper[2] suggests that the average trust's TER is around 1.3 per cent, compared with 1.6 per cent for open-ended funds. Nearly a third of trusts have TERs of less than 1 per cent. Indeed, many charge much less – their TER being little more than that of passive funds such as index-trackers or exchange-traded funds (ETFs). The investment trust average is raised by trusts focusing on specialist areas such as property, infrastructure or hedge funds, which charge higher fees because of the nature of the investments. But despite such trusts expanding in number, the Association of Investment Companies has still found that on average expense ratios are falling (see Table 2.3).

But the total costs of investing do not stop there. For TERs do not include hidden charges such as dealing costs, stamp duty, research costs and entry or exit charges. And these extra hidden charges can be significant. One or two insiders have suggested that the average annual turnover (the extent to which a fund manager changes the portfolio) on a typical unit trust is around 50 per cent: in other words, the portfolio is changed completely once every two years.

Table 2.3   **The 10 cheapest investment trusts in 2011**

Investment trust	TER(%)	TER inc performance fee (%)
Independent IT	0.36	0.36
Edinburgh US Tracker Trust	0.4	0.4
Bankers*	0.42	0.42
Law Debenture Corporation*	0.49	0.49
City of London*	0.49	0.5
Mercantile	0.55	0.55
Henderson Smaller Cos*	0.56	0.56
Scottish Mortgage	0.56	0.56
Temple Bar	0.56	0.56
Electric & General*	0.62	0.65
British Assets Trust*	0.62	0.74

* Trust which has a performance fee in place
Source: From Walters, L. (2011), 'Investment fees on the rise', *Investors Chronicle*, 3–9 June.

The wealth management firm Spencer-Churchill Miller (SCM Private) says that these further charges bring the total cost of investing in the average UK unit trust up to 2.8 per cent a year, rather than the often quoted TER of around 1.6 per cent. The sum of £10,000 invested over 10 years and producing a 7 per cent a year return would grow to £16,761 with a fund charging 1.6 per cent. However, if the total cost of investing was actually 2.8 per cent then this return would decrease to £14,862 – a decrease of £1,899.

The Millers, a husband and wife team who run SCM, certainly believe that if investors were fully aware of all costs then they would make very different investment decisions – and the industry would be forced to bring down costs. Such findings are confirmed by other studies. John Lang and the economist Kevin James have shown separately that hidden charges add around 1 per cent to the TER of an average unit trust.

Some in the industry are trying to address the issue – to make fees more transparent. For example, Fidelity has proposed a new figure called the total cost of ownership (TCO). This would include the fund manager's fee, administrative charges, dealing costs and stamp duty, together with the costs of distribution and advice. This would be a much fairer reflection of the true costs borne by the client. SCM has suggested something similar.

Of course, whatever the chosen method, there is no precise way of measuring these extra costs, if only because fund managers can and do vary the extent they change their portfolios from one year to the next. Any number of factors can affect turnover, including market conditions and company-specific news. Although evidence would suggest the more successful fund managers tend to have lower turnovers, investors should not seek to dictate how their money is being managed.

Even when it comes to turnover, once again investment trusts have an advantage over their open-ended cousins. Being closed-ended, investors are trading the shares and not the portfolio, which therefore remains unaffected. By contrast, open-ended funds that see inflows or outflows of money, particularly if large, will see higher turnover in the underlying portfolio to match these money flows even if holdings are not being changed.

The message remains the same: be aware of the costs of investing and how this can affect portfolio performance, and remember that investment trusts look to be the better deal.

Performance fees and Warren Buffett

Some managers charge performance fees on top of the annual management charges. These can take various forms, but the theory is the same: a fee that rises with improved performance helps to align the interests of investors and managers alike.

It sounds good, but the case has not been proved. There is little difference in performance between funds charging performance fees and those that do not when looking at the 12-month returns of the IMA absolute return category.

This is one reason why the number of open-ended funds using performance fees has been in decline in recent years. There are now around 80 such funds – just 3 per cent of the entire UK funds universe. By contrast, Lipper has confirmed that around half of investment trusts still use performance fees.

According to Lipper, another reason for the demise of performance fees is the 'Hargreaves Lansdown effect'. Hargreaves Lansdown is a major and reputable independent financial services provider that has regularly attacked the concept of performance fees. Scepticism from such UK intermediaries has resulted in fewer funds imposing performance fees (see Table 2.4).

TABLE 2.4   Funds launched with performance fees, to September 2012

Year	Number of funds
2004	5
2005	7
2006	19
2007	13
2008	17
2009	18
2010	12
2011	6
2012	2

Source: From O'Neill, M. (2012), 'Performance fees in decline', *Investors Chronicle*, 14–20 September.

While it is fair to say that performance fees can work well in the interests of investors, there is a wide variety of structures in place. So investors need to examine the detail closely. For example, some fee structures encourage fund managers to increase or decrease the risk profile of the portfolio regardless of the investment opportunities on offer. To counter this, a performance fee should have a high water mark so that such considerations do not typically enter the mix. It should also be calculated against the average performance achieved over a three to five year timeframe to encourage long-term investing.

As to whether managers should be rewarded when beating the index but not cash, or penalised when they underperform to the same extent they are rewarded when they outperform, investors should be aware that there are several views.

I suggest managers should only be paid when they outperform their benchmarks, having charged for covering essential running costs – this latter charge being capped so that investors do not pay more simply because the underlying portfolios have increased in value beyond a certain point. This would be the best way of aligning the interests of investors and managers, whilst acknowledging that managers do have legitimate administrative costs.

One of the best examples of this approach is that of Warren Buffett when he ran his own investment business. His water mark was 6 per cent. He did not get paid any fee until he had produced a 6 per cent performance. He then retained 25 per cent of any return in excess of 6 per cent, subject to an agreed minimum. Therefore, if the fund produced a 14 per cent return, the investor would get 12 per cent and Buffett 2 per cent.

Having shared the gain, Buffett would also share the pain. Any returns less than 6 per cent would have to be earned or made up in future years before he could take his fee. A bad year could not simply be written off – the manager and investor would both suffer. Furthermore, Buffett believed a manager should invest a significant proportion of their own money into the fund to help focus attention.

There must be few better ways of ensuring the interests of investors and managers are matched and it would perhaps encourage managers to adopt a different approach when investing. First, they would focus on not losing money or falling behind the agreed water mark for fear of having to make up lost ground in future years. But it would also encourage managers to focus more on investing in undervalued companies and less on copying the benchmark or index.

This is not a popular suggestion. Despite – or because of – its attractions to investors, many fund management groups would not survive under such a fee structure. There would be a downsizing of the industry or, to be more precise, a downsizing of the 'active' fund management sector. Investors could still invest in cheap index-trackers such as ETFs to keep pace with markets. But they would also have the added option of paying for active fund management.

There is, of course, no perfect answer when it comes to charging structures, but at least the above method would ensure investors got what they paid for – good performance and managers acting in their interests. The future belongs to those fund management groups who adopt such a method, and who then perform well.

3

The opportunities and risks of discounts

Better performance and cheaper fees are two powerful reasons why investment trusts should be favoured. But there is a host of other advantages (and some disadvantages) to these trusts which are largely ignored or misunderstood by both professional advisers and investors alike. The discount is chief among them.

Opportunities and risks

Buying something at a discount to its true value is a national pastime – we all love a bargain. Buying investments should be no different, yet the majority of investors do not take advantage of this generous offer from investment trusts.

As investors know, unlike open-ended funds, an investment trust's share price can deviate from the net asset value (NAV) of the underlying portfolio. The price is influenced by investor demand, whereas the NAV reflects the value of the portfolio. When the share price is below the NAV, the trust is said to be *at a discount*. Most trusts trade at a discount. A 10 per cent discount means that investors are paying 90p for shares when the assets (the NAV) are worth 100p. But trusts can also trade at premiums, when the share price exceeds NAV.

Changes to the discounts or premiums of these trusts present both opportunities and risks for the investor. A discount that narrows or a premium that expands helps shareholders because the share price has risen faster (or fallen less) than the NAV. Conversely, a widening discount or contracting premium is unhelpful as the share price falls further behind its NAV (see Figure 3.1).

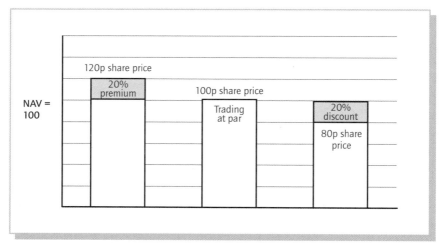

Figure 3.1   **Price relative to NAV**

Furthermore, because of fluctuations in the discount, an investor does not know how much others will pay for their shares even though the NAV is known. This contrasts with open-ended funds where the share price is firmly rooted to the NAV.

We shall look at both the opportunities and risks in a little more detail later in the chapter, but first we need to better understand the factors that affect discounts, and why individual trusts trade at the discounts they do. This is important when making investment decisions because it helps investors to balance the opportunities and risks.

Factors affecting discounts

A variety of reasons helps to explain why most trusts trade at a discount, and why changes in the discount level occur.

One is ignorance. Because investment trusts are a little more complex and therefore less understood than unit trusts and open-ended investment companies (OEICs), and because they have not yet entered the investment mainstream, there is understandably an element of caution. Because discounts can and do exist, and with them concurrent volatility, some advisers view trusts as 'risky' and therefore best avoided. This is reflected in share prices. If trusts were better understood, then extra investor demand would push up prices and narrow the discount.

Another is performance and with it demand. Investors understandably do not wish to own those trusts that are not performing well. More sellers than buyers weigh on the share price which then falls relative to NAV, and so the discount widens. The discount may then stay wide for some time until performance improves.

But it is interesting to note that those fund managers who have consistently good long-term track records tend to be rewarded by the market with discounts close to NAV, or even with premiums. This is true even in those sectors where decent discounts are the norm: for example, Standard Life UK Smaller Companies Trust (SLI) is standing close to NAV, compared to a sector average discount of 15 per cent.

Additionally, sentiment regarding the future prospects of a sector or region can move discounts regardless of the past performance of the relevant trusts. The future is more important than the past. Discounts can narrow when investors get excited about prospects and buy the shares, and widen when they fear the worst and sell.

Investor demand may not just reflect performance or sentiment. In this low-interest environment where good-quality yield is hard to find, premiums often exist in those trusts offering a decent and safe yield – even for those where NAV performance has simply been acceptable, rather than exceptional. Examples include trusts within the UK Income Growth, Global Income Growth and Infrastructure sectors, although some trusts within these sectors have performed exceptionally well.

Another factor affecting discounts can be the quality of communication between the trust and shareholders. If the trust's management is not good at marketing and communicating long-term strategy, and explaining why buying and selling decisions are made, then shareholders are unnecessarily in the dark.

Trusts can perhaps get away with this when things are going well and the NAV keeps rising, but share prices tend to suffer when the shocks come along as they invariably do. Shareholders who understand and believe in the strategy, and know the trust well, will tend to hold and not sell their shares when times are tricky. Trusts have become better at understanding the importance of good communication and many now have monthly web-based factsheets to update investors as to progress. A host of other information is available on these websites, including the report and accounts, and all are well worth a read.

Many other reasons can and do affect discounts. For example, the make-up of the shareholder list is sometimes important. Those trusts that have a large individual private client shareholder base relative to their institutional shareholders tend to have narrower discounts. This is often because private investors are longer-term investors and so hang on to their shares through thick and thin, perhaps encouraged by capital gains tax considerations if decent gains exist.

A change in fund manager or strategy can also affect investor demand and therefore discounts. News of the appointment of a new manager with a good track record elsewhere can narrow the wide discount of a hitherto lacklustre trust. Conversely, a successful manager leaving can result in selling pressure and discounts widening if there are doubts about the incoming manager's track record or ability.

A change in strategy can also affect the discount and this happens more than investors may think. Investment trusts have rightly adapted to changing circumstances over the years. Part of the job of the independent board is to review trust policies and strategy, and introduce change where it is felt necessary. 2011 saw 11 trusts change their investment policies in response to challenging times – up from five the previous year.

Association of Investment Companies (AIC) data suggest that one theme influencing these changes is that trusts have broadened their scope globally. For example, the Martin Currie Global Portfolio (MNP) had been benchmarked against the UK's FTSE All-Share index, but now measures itself against the FTSE World index. The hunt for income remains another key theme in this low-interest environment, and again trusts are now extending their search into overseas markets for that yield – a theme we will pick up in later chapters. The level of the discount is affected depending on how well the change is perceived by the market.

Big picture strategy decisions aside, day-to-day management decisions can also have a marginal effect on the discount. One example is when a manager changes the level of gearing – the level of debt carried by the trust – even within the tolerances set by the board of directors. Increased gearing has the effect of accentuating the movement of the underlying assets. This can deter or encourage investors depending on their outlook on the market.

Another factor can be market volatility – particularly when markets fall. Like other public companies, investment trusts can be traded every minute that markets are open – whereas open-ended funds are usually traded once a day, with the order having to be placed by mid-day for the price to be known the following day. When bad days come along, some investors want to sell immediately regardless of NAV movements. This is possible with investment trusts but not with open-ended funds, and discounts often widen as a result. An additional factor is, of course, the level of gearing which can accentuate this volatility.

In short, all sorts of factors affect the extent of discounts. But it is the fact that discounts exist which presents the opportunities.

How to judge value

Investors should always be seeking discount value when it comes to monitoring investment trust portfolios: to 'prune' portfolios by constantly asking whether existing holdings look expensive relative to potential alternatives, and thereby conversely questioning whether potential holdings look cheap by comparison. A host of factors needs to be considered.

You should always compare apples with apples – trusts within the same sector or geographic region. An investor needs to get a feel as to what the sector or region discount average is, which will help to put a trust's discount into perspective. But seeking value is not just about a simple comparison of discounts.

Do not base investment decisions purely on the extent of a trust's discount. If the discount is significantly different to its sector average or to its own recent average, then there is a good reason. Performance is the usual answer but it may also be other factors, as already discussed, such as communication, a change of manager or strategy, etc. Such factors may be valid, in which case the trust's discount or premium – out of sync though it apparently is – may remain in place for a long time.

However, anomalies can and do exist. Some trusts do represent better value than others over the longer term, and switches are worthwhile. For example, the market can be lazy and sometimes brand trusts in an unfashionable sector with the same wide discount – even the better-performing ones. Likewise, the market often attributes premiums to trusts which are difficult to justify or simply wrong. Investors should seek such opportunities.

One of the best strategies with investment trusts is to buy a good fund manager who is temporarily out of favour because of a difficult patch in performance, preferably in a sector that is also out of favour, and then tuck this away for the longer term. Patient investors are usually disproportionately rewarded in the trust sector, helped by the wide discounts created by impatient investors.

Seeking value is also about comparing discounts and premiums *relative* to performance. Sometimes, premiums are justified if performance is consistently ahead of the peer group. A good example is Jupiter European Opportunities Trust (JEO) which stands at a premium despite the sector average, including smaller companies, standing at a 10 per cent discount. This is justified given its vastly superior performance over the years. Wider discounts may exist, but this is rarely an opportunity if these trusts' relative performance is poor by comparison.

However, it should always be remembered that the importance of discounts, relative to performance, wanes with time. The quality of the product as reflected in its good performance is what really matters over time. As with life generally, quality will be remembered long after price is forgotten. Discount considerations should no more than help to time long-term changes in portfolios, and not short-term trading opportunities which will typically raise costs and hit performance.

Speculating over the short term requires constant discount monitoring. Getting the market direction right is also important. It is difficult to make money if the NAV is heading in the wrong direction, regardless of movements in the discount. But if the objective is long-term investment, then performance considerations are paramount. Pick a good fund manager and, within reason and over time, the discount matters much less – especially as consistently good performance is rewarded with tighter discounts or even premiums. It is wise to monitor changes in fund managers for this reason.

The risks of investment trusts

Opportunities and risks are usually travelling companions. Just as the fact that discounts exist can present opportunities, they can also present dangers to the unwary shareholder.

Discounts widen when the share price falls further behind the NAV, whether in a rising or falling market. In a rising market, shareholders may feel no pain at all because the share price will often go up even if the discount widens. Where discounts can really hurt shareholders is when they widen in a falling market – the NAV fall is magnified by the share price falling further.

And investment trust discounts do widen when markets are going through a rough patch or are very volatile. This tends to be because investors can deal in these trusts every minute the market is open – subject to the size of the trust and hence its marketability. When investors get scared about markets, they can and do sell the shares without knowing precisely how the underlying portfolio is performing relative to the market fallout. By comparison, unit trust prices – calculated just once a day – usually better reflect their NAV.

Meanwhile, those who determine the prices in these trusts – the market makers – anticipate this wave of selling. They often mark down prices before the selling materialises and/or limit marketability by reducing the number of shares in which they are prepared to deal. This is perfectly legitimate, if somewhat annoying for investors. The same happens to shares in other listed companies.

It can all add up to be a bloody affair. But we should remember that these market sell-offs also tend to be short-term affairs. Given the out-performance of investment trust NAVs over the longer term, and their many other advantages, it is no surprise that discounts on average have narrowed somewhat in recent years. Recent developments, such as the change to paying dividends out of capital and the introduction of the Retail Distribution Review, may see this trend continue.

But even if such factors have little effect, it is the portfolio performance that looks set to continue to dictate the level of discounts. And this is absolutely logical and right – for investors should always focus on the long term.

Discount control mechanisms

The average discount across the sector at present is around 8 per cent, but there are large variances between sectors and trusts. Furthermore, discounts add a layer of volatility to share prices – these prices being influenced by investor demand, sometimes irrespective of movements in the NAV, which can therefore make for fluctuations in the discount. Accordingly, in recent years there have been increasing efforts by invest-ments trusts to reduce the discounts and hence the volatility. The theory is that this should help to reduce the risk factor for shareholders and so make the shares more attractive to own, with prices reacting accordingly.

Often the investment trust will publicly make it known that it has a discount control policy in place to limit the extent of the discount – the 'discount trigger' – and give an indication as to its level. Trusts achieve this by buying back their own shares in the market from existing share-holders using surplus cash. These shares are then cancelled or retained and then re-issued at a higher price if market conditions allow. Other public companies do likewise as a way of enhancing returns, using cash that would otherwise lie relatively dormant.

By reducing the number of shares, the trust is increasing the NAV per share because the number of shares in the market has been reduced. Such a policy also creates demand or at least clears an overhang of stock. Investors should check whether a discount control mechanism is in place with existing or potential holdings (see Table 3.1).

| Table 3.1 | Trusts with discount control policies |

Investment trust	Discount trigger (%)
Aberdeen All Asia	12.0
Aberdeen Asian Income	5.0
Aberdeen Latin American Income	5.0
Aberdeen New Thai	15.0
Baring Emerging Europe	12.0
BH Macro	5.0
Biotech Growth	6.0
BlackRock Latin American	13.5
Dunedin Smaller Companies	7.5
European Assets	5.0
F&C Commercial Property	5.0
F&C Global Smaller Companies	5.0
F&C Managed Portfolio Growth	5.0
F&C Managed Portfolio Income	5.0
F&C US Smaller Companies	10.0
Finsbury Growth & Income	5.0
Foreign & Colonial	10.0
Henderson Asian Growth	10.0
Henderson European Focus	3.5
Henderson EuroTrust	5.0
Henderson Global	8.0
Henderson Private Equity	5.0
Inv Perp Select Global Equity Income	4.0
Inv Perp Select UK Equity	4.0
JPMorgan Brazil	5.0

Investment trust	Discount trigger (%)
JPMorgan Emerging Markets	10.0
JPMorgan Emerging Growth	10.0
JPMorgan European Income	10.0
JPMorgan Overseas	5.0
JPMorgan Russian Securities	8.0
JPMorgan US Smaller Companies	10.0
Jupiter Primadona Growth	8.0
Martin Currie Global Portfolio	7.5
Midas Income & Growth	5.0
Miton Worldwide Growth	3.0
Personal Assets Trust	0.0
Schroder Oriental Income	5.0
Schroder UK Growth	5.0
Scottish Investment Trust	9.0
Securities Trust of Scotland	7.5
Standard Life UK Smaller Companies	5.0
Troy Income & Growth	0.0
Witan	10.0

Source: From St. George, R. (2012), 'When the price isn't right', *What Investment.*

The mechanism itself is simple. Trusts buy back their own shares in one of two ways. The first is a simple purchase in the market. The trust benefits from the discount by purchasing the shares cheaply. The second is a tender, when the trust offers to buy shares slightly above the market price. Shareholders benefit, whilst this policy allows the board of directors to highlight its confidence in the trust to the market. Opinions differ as to which method is best. BlackRock's Greater Europe Trust extends a tender offer to its shareholders every six months, offering to buy shares at 98 per cent of NAV. This appears to have succeeded in keeping the discount very narrow. Others prefer the open market buyback.

There is of course no guarantee that the discount trigger level will be attained and held, for this is not an exact science and other factors such as market conditions are at play. However, whichever method is chosen, the policy has tended to work regardless of scale. Alliance Trust, the largest investment trust, significantly reduced its discount in 2011 – in one 24-hour period from 28 per cent to 20 per cent – by buying back a record level of shares, because of pressure from shareholders concerned by the wide discount. The trust now trades at a 15 per cent discount.

However, one downside with discount control mechanisms is that they can raise the TER. Buybacks reduce the number of shares in existence and therefore the capital base of the fund, which means the fixed running costs become proportionately higher. This is less of a problem for larger trusts than it is for smaller ones. Indeed, the assets of small trusts have been known to fall to such a level that the board has decided the TER is too great a burden, and have therefore handed the assets back to shareholders.

There is no definitive guide, but I suggest trusts with assets of less than £50 million are approaching the level at which these considerations become meaningful. The implication from this being that these trusts are unlikely to instigate discount control mechanisms, and wide discounts lasting a long time may be the consequence – something to consider if one is thinking of buying.

Another factor affecting buybacks is the level of liquidity within each trust. Buying back shares draws on the trust's cash and sometimes – because the cupboard is bare – assets have to be sold to fund these purchases. This can be a problem for a trust with illiquid assets such as property or private equity. So these types of trusts tend not to have discount mechanisms in place, for fear of becoming a forced seller of assets – never a good idea.

Finally, if a discount control policy is in place, the trust's board needs to decide whether it should establish a fixed policy, known as a 'hard' discount control mechanism, or retain some flexibility. Opinions are divided. Foreign & Colonial (F&C) Investment Trust operates the former whenever the discount exceeds 10 per cent. Before this policy was adopted it had operated a different one, but believes the present policy serves both shareholders and the trust well. There can be little doubt that certainty benefits shareholders – if only as to the timing of purchases should, for example, the discount for F&C be wider than 10 per cent.

However, there are disadvantages with the 'hard' discount mechanism. Short-term calculations relative to the discount threshold can drive demand, rather than longer-term investment considerations. And it is usually the large institutions that benefit from arbitraging the difference between NAVs and discounts, rather than the private investor.

In conclusion, buybacks work well when used sensibly. A trust's discount relative to its sector average is a factor – defending a 10 per cent limit when the average discount is double that, would be difficult to justify. But on balance, the evidence suggests they work because they lessen discounts and hence price volatility, help provide liquidity and reassure shareholders that a backstop is in place.

4

Other pros and cons of investment trusts

The tendency of investment trusts to outperform both open-ended funds and the benchmarks – a performance assisted by cheaper fees – is a powerful reason for investors to favour them. The opportunity presented by fluctuations in the discount is another, although the risks need to be understood. But there are other pros and cons that you also need to understand.

Investment trusts are better understood

Despite investment trusts being the earliest form of mutual fund, loved by a small circle of investors both professional and private, they are neither well known nor widely recommended by independent financial advisers (IFAs).

Historically, IFAs and some investors have viewed investment trusts with suspicion, believing them to be more volatile and complex than their open-ended cousins, and therefore more risky. This is of course partly true. Discounts do increase the volatility of share prices, and the structure of trusts is more complex. But this does not make trusts more risky.

In fact, the situation is quite the reverse. We have seen in previous chapters how investment trusts perform better, assisted by cheaper fees. If you are investing over the longer term, then the effects of volatility are neutralised and there really is no better investment vehicle. Indeed, investors need to remember that if volatility is a measure of risk, then in shunning volatility they will always be underweight good opportunities. As an investor, you should learn how to embrace it. Volatility can be exploited by investors to help time their deals.

As to trusts' so-called complexity, this is again overplayed. Trusts are no more complex than any other quoted company such as Shell or Marks & Spencer. Their structure is the same. They have a board of directors whose members monitor how well the management is looking after the assets. This management can take day-to-day operational decisions, such as buying or selling assets and increasing borrowings, with the aim of enhancing shareholder value. In many ways, this structure adds to their attraction.

What is needed is a better understanding of the merits of investment trusts – both by advisers and investors alike.

This is where the Retail Distribution Review (RDR), which was enacted in January 2013, may have a profound effect. As we know, the RDR has banned trailing commissions from open-ended funds to IFAs: this should allow investment trusts to compete on a more level playing field. But the Financial Services Authority (FSA) has also made it clear in the RDR that investment trusts should now be included in the full spectrum of retail investment products considered by IFAs.

This is good news, because the better education of professional advisers can only benefit investors. Both initiatives – related but separate – will help trusts become better understood.

Whichever route investors now take to accessing markets, it should lead them to trusts. If you employ an IFA or wealth manager, they will want the better investment vehicles most suited to their objectives. In addition, the IFAs – through better training because of the RDR – will be better able to help. If, on the other hand, investors manage their own portfolios then, with the help of the media and I hope books like this, their investigations should unearth the treasure that is trusts.

Either way, investors will benefit – just as clients of City wealth managers have for decades.

Gearing

Like other public companies, investment trusts are free to borrow subject to any restrictions agreed with their board of directors. By contrast, open-ended funds are restricted by regulations and so cannot. Borrowing can work both ways of course. But a good trust that is geared will produce enhanced returns when markets are rising.

> ### Example
>
> As an example, let's assume that there are two trusts – A and B – each with £100 million under management (see Table 4.1). A is positive about markets and so decides to borrow £30 million and buys stocks with this money. B is less convinced and doesn't borrow. The market then rises 40 per cent over a period of time. A then decides to pay back its borrowings by selling some of its stock. Assuming A's performance matches the market, the portfolio will therefore be worth £152 million (£130 million × 140 per cent = £182 million, minus £30 million repayment of debt). B's portfolio, on the other hand, will be worth £140 million (£100 million x 140 per cent). Shareholders in A's trust benefit through an enhanced net asset value (NAV).

Table 4.1	Performance of two trusts (A and B) each with £100 million under management (all figures in £ million)					
Trust	Portfolio value	Borrowings	Invested in market	Portfolio value after 40% market rise	Debt repaid	Portfolio end value
A	100	30	130	182	−30	152
B	100	0	100	140	0	140

In reality, investment trusts do not usually gear up by as much as 30 per cent, but the example illustrates the point. Managers can gear their portfolios in a variety of ways, but typically gearing is executed via fixed-term borrowings that need to be redeemed by a certain point. Flexible borrowing has become more common, such as short-term bank credit, in the low-interest environment. But whichever method is chosen, increased borrowing can enhance share price performance as it accentuates movements in the underlying NAV. If the gearing has benefited the portfolio, borrowings can then be repaid from the enhanced profits.

But of course it can work the opposite way. Just as gearing can magnify profits on the way up, it can also magnify losses on the way down. And the losses to NAV can of course be magnified further if share prices are hit by a widening discount.

As an investor, you may be reassured to know that there are safeguards in place. Managers cannot just borrow what they please. Restrictions as to the extent of borrowing are stipulated by the independent board of directors and confirmed by shareholders at the annual general meeting. Should managers wish to borrow beyond the agreed limits then they have to seek permission – and justify their requests. The board of directors will scrutinise proposals on behalf of shareholders and make the appropriate recommendation to shareholders. Meanwhile, they will be monitoring the manager's use of the existing debt facility.

But gearing can also be unhelpful in other ways. If an investment trust is heavily geared, with various layers of debt, then this can make for complexity, which can put investors off. Even analysts can sometimes struggle to quantify how such debt can affect portfolio performance under different market scenarios – particularly if the debt is multi-tiered and being serviced at different interest rates.

An example of this is Ecofin Water & Power Opportunities Trust (ECWO). This trust has a high and growing dividend yield of 5.5 per cent, a good quality portfolio and invests in global utilities, which are considered 'defensive' or safe relative to other 'more sexy' sectors of the equity market. And yet it still stands on a more than 20 per cent discount in 2013. But the level of gearing and complex capital structure (see later chapters) is perceived to have added a level of risk which shareholders need compensating for by what appears to be a wide discount.

I say wide discount but debt, in effect, reduces the portfolio value and therefore NAV. If markets go sideways and the portfolio stays static, then in reality the portfolio is reduced in value by the value of that debt. The debt only becomes a positive factor if the portfolio rises. Worse still, if the percentage interest rate on that debt exceeds the percentage gain on the portfolio, then a further negative factor is added to the mix. This negative multiplies if the portfolio goes down in value.

All in all, you must be aware of the level of debt carried by investment trusts. In the vast majority of cases, it is relatively benign. Those trusts which are geared are usually by no more than say 10–15 per cent. However, a minority well and truly exceed this and, the market being aware, can trade on what appear wide discounts and therefore look cheap.

Always look under the bonnet. Most brokers' lists or publications highlight gearing, but you should not buy without knowing the facts and always keep an eye on changes. Investment trusts do need a little more monitoring than open-ended funds for this reason. We will touch upon gearing again when we cover split-capital trusts in the next chapter.

Directors and shareholders

Like other public companies, investment trusts have an independent board of directors whose brief is to represent shareholders' interests. And these directors have teeth. They can, for example, with shareholder approval, fire an underperforming manager and move the trust to another fund management house – something I have never heard of in the unit trust industry!

It is true to say that, in the past, investment trust boards have been accused of having too close a relationship with their fund managers, or for being a bit too sleepy. This has changed a lot in the past decade. The more professional composition of boards has helped, and now the vast majority do a good job on behalf of shareholders. And so they should because, being a listed company, it is the shareholders who own the trust. The directors are there at the shareholders' behest, and their salaries are drawn from the assets of the trust.

A related but separate bonus is the fact that, being a public company, shareholders have significant powers. For a start, they can vote on issues such as changes to investment policy and the appointment of directors. They can turn up at shareholder meetings and ask awkward questions, typically about remuneration and the introduction or alteration of performance-related fees. It is, after all, their company.

This leads to a much more transparent environment – certainly more so when compared to closed-ended funds. As such, the concept 'survival of the fittest' prevails and is certainly strongest in the investment trust sector. Because of its much larger size, it is easier for lacklustre funds to survive in the open-ended universe. Not so with investment trusts. Shareholder agitation, both private but usually the larger institutions, will challenge investment trusts where performance is mediocre or poor and/or discounts are consistently wide. Trusts can be closed down or managements changed as a result.

This is what happened to the Eaglet Trust in 2008. This trust had suffered from a consistently wide discount, which it had failed to narrow despite some pressure from shareholders. So activist investors replaced the manager – it then became known as the Directors' Dealing Investment Trust. The following year, the trust's biggest shareholder then forced a second change and replaced the manager with Midas.

The possibility of management change, proven over time, is in share-holders' best interests. Investment trusts are on notice. Trusts need to do what they reasonably can to enhance shareholder returns through good performance, low fees, efficient use of gearing, and reduced discounts and volatility.

The long term and alternative assets

Because unit trusts and open-ended investment trusts (OEICs) are open-ended and so portfolio size is affected by investors' demand for their shares, their managers have to buy and sell holdings as money flows in and out of the portfolio. This may not always be the right investment decision. Some investors sell their unit trust holdings after market falls, when in fact they should be buying. The fund managers may also think so, but may be forced to sell because they have no choice – redemptions have to be met. Conversely, managers may have to buy holdings after a strong market run, against their better judgement. This can hinder per-formance over time.

Investment trust managers do not suffer from this pressure. They buy and sell when they – and not the investor – think the time is right. The structure of investment trusts helps good fund managers make better investment decisions. The structure makes it easier for managers to take a long-term approach to the market, not influenced by short-term market fluctuations or money flows which can encourage short-term decisions. This is a contributory factor as to why trusts tend to outperform not only unit trusts, but also the 'mirror' open-ended funds run by the same manager.

And because trust managers do not have to worry about meeting redemptions and therefore can take longer-term decisions, the universe of investible assets widens.

Less liquid assets such as very small companies, commercial property, private equity and infrastructure projects – investments which by their very nature can involve time horizons of several years – are better suited to the structure of investment trusts. The managers running these portfolios are better able to invest in such assets for the benefit of their shareholders, knowing they can take a long-term view in line with their investments.

Of course, shareholders in these sorts of trusts are not locked in. They can sell the shares when they like. Investment trusts therefore solve one of the key problems for many alternative assets in that investors can buy or sell the shares in the same way as any other listed share, and not have to wait for lengthy lock-up periods to expire. For this reason, trusts have benefited both these alternative assets and their investors alike.

Size and marketability

Investment trusts tend to be on average smaller than open-ended funds. I believe this makes it easier for them to focus on their objectives because they do not become too large and unwieldy. Trusts require shareholder approval if they wish to grow beyond their initial remit. Many also have a fixed life, which again requires shareholder approval to extend.

Conversely, the size of open-ended funds fluctuates with investor demand. Large funds can work – big can be beautiful – because economies of scale can kick in for the benefit of shareholders in the form of lower relative costs and better buying power. But evidence suggests that open-ended funds find it harder to replicate their past performance the larger they become, possibly because the investment process loses its focus.

Some assets are best managed in smaller funds. The smaller company sector is one example. Dealing in size is often not possible because such companies are often illiquid or difficult to deal in a reasonable size. Large portfolios, whether open- or closed-ended, would therefore typically need to have lots of small holdings. This can make such portfolios more difficult to monitor.

When it comes to the marketability – the ability to deal in the market – of the investment trust or the open-ended fund, two factors should be considered.

1   Being a publicly listed company, the shares of an investment trust can usually be traded easily and frequently without restrictions. They can be bought and sold every minute the market is open. This is not the case with unit trusts where deals are placed the day before, usually by mid-day, in advance of knowing the next day's price. A lot can happen in that time, but the process cannot be rushed.

2   Unit trusts are usually easier to deal in size. Small investment trusts – as with very small public companies generally – can be somewhat illiquid and therefore difficult to deal.

But liquidity can mean different things to different people. The average investor will have no trouble in dealing in the vast majority of investment trusts. According to WINS Investment Trusts, when it comes to the nine largest trusts with a market capitalisation exceeding £1 billion, the average trading activity in a day is just under £2.5 million. Even the average trust sees just over £300,000 of shares traded each day – more than enough for the average investor.

Where problems may be encountered is when firms of wealth managers and private client brokers trade investment trusts *en bloc* across a swathe of their clients. Managers increasingly construct core lists of trust portfolios in order to ensure consistency of performance and proper monitoring of holdings. These lists will vary depending on such factors as the risk tolerance of the client, the level of income required and the choice of base currency.

But the principle is the same – in the majority of cases, core lists are adhered to once a client's individual requirements have been identified and the appropriate list assigned. The days have largely gone when fund managers sitting next to each other could be trading in opposite directions. Things have been tightened up. The process encourages research rigour and risk control, and clients have benefited.

Once a trust is to be traded, it is usually in size and may take a number of days to execute. The size can be a couple of million pounds. There are no consistent guidelines but, as a rough rule of thumb, many wealth management companies are unlikely to invest clients' money in trusts with a market capitalisation of much less than £50 million. Otherwise, liquidity can be a problem. It is no surprise then that the larger investment trusts tend to feature on these lists.

Some investment trusts help the situation by issuing more shares when standing at a premium to NAV. The underlying portfolio increases in size through the issuance of these extra shares, which are usually priced at a slight reduction to the prevailing premium at the time. Short term this can have the effect of lowering the premium as more shares hit the market and satisfy investor demand. Longer term, such a policy should reduce running costs and the total expense ratio (TER) as the costs of running this larger portfolio are no different to before. This should benefit existing and new shareholders, if only marginally.

But there are a few investment trusts which, because of their size (market capitalisation), will usually present difficulties for the average investor. These are the very small trusts with market capitalisations of usually less than £30 million to £40 million. Think about the difficulty in dealing before investing – especially as this difficulty increases significantly in turbulent markets, just when you may want to deal to get out!

Such smaller-sized trusts, particularly if rarely traded, can often have their price moved by the smallest of trades. It is not always easy to buy or sell at prices that suit you. But if you wish to deal in such a trust, then it is usually best to leave the deal with your broker or online provider, having set a limit order so you do not overpay. If you wish to deal in size, then holdings usually have to be bought or sold over a number of deals and/ or periods of time.

At this stage, we should also remember that some open-ended funds are also difficult to deal. Restrictions can exist as to when in the week they can be traded, and some can even close without notice to new money because of size. Difficulty in dealing can exist for both open- and closed-ended funds, and is a function of the market.

Dividends

One of the most attractive features of investment trusts is their ability to retain up to 15% of dividends and income received from holdings in the underlying portfolio, in any one year. This 'surplus cash' is called the revenue reserve, and it is always worth checking the level of reserves particularly if you are investing for income. For me, the best way of quantifying it is by expressing it as a period over which the existing dividend could be maintained if there were suddenly no dividends generated by the portfolio. Advisers will say, for example, that reserves cover one year of dividends.

Table 4.2 shows how revenue reserves tables are usually portrayed. The second column of the table gives the annual cost of each trust's total dividend. The third column shows the total revenue reserves that have been accumulated over the years for each trust. The final column shows the third column divided by the second, and then expressed as a percentage: 100 per cent denotes that the revenue reserves cover one year's dividend. Such tables are usually broken down by peer group, such as UK Income Growth.

Table 4.2	Revenue reserves		
Investment trust	Total cost of this year's dividend (£m)	Revenue reserves accumulated (£m)	Cover (%)
A	42.9	60.4	141
B	23.7	23.7	100
C	3.1	2.4	77

These reserves can be used to supplement future dividend payments. Money is put aside in the good times. Such a strategy is helpful when economic times are tough and the companies held in portfolios are having trouble increasing their dividends. In such times, investment trusts – especially those with a brief to produce a decent level of income – have increased their dividends to their shareholders by drawing upon these reserves.

Some investment trusts have very proud histories when it comes to growing dividends. The trusts with the longest records are highlighted in Table 4.3. City of London, Alliance Trust and Bankers Investment Trust have all increased dividends for 46 consecutive years – quite a record. But where revenue reserves and records become particularly important is with those trusts that strive to produce a decent income for their share-holders. Safety and growth are key objectives.

Table 4.3   **Dividend heroes**

Investment trust	Number of consecutive years dividend increased
City of London	46
Alliance Trust	46
Bankers Investment Trust	46
Caledonia Investments	45
Foreign & Colonial	42
F&C Global Smaller Companies	42
Brunner	41
JPMorgan Claverhouse	40

What the table shows: the investment trusts that have increased their actual dividend per share for the greatest number of years in a row. Trusts are all from the AIC's Global Growth sector except City of London and JPMorgan Claverhouse (UK Growth).

Source: From *What Investment*, March 2013.

Another advantage with decent-yielding investment trusts is when they are standing at a discount to NAV. The trust's portfolio is producing an income which the shareholder is getting at a discount. Let us say a portfolio is yielding 10p a share, which is a yield of 5 per cent on a share price of 200p. If the price were to drop to 160p, then the underlying portfolio would still be producing the same level of income and so the yield becomes 6.25 per cent (i.e. 10 divided by 160). The same is true of public companies generally, except that investment trusts have a greater ability to grow dividends in hard times if reserves permit.

Capital changes

New legislation effective from 6 April 2012 could enhance the dividend attractions of investments trusts even further. Prior to this, they could only pay dividends to the limit their revenue reserves allowed. Investment trusts will now be allowed to dip into their capital – crystallising gains from the underlying portfolio – in order to supplement their dividend-paying ability.

This could have a number of advantages. Those managers with an income brief could become less constrained in their stock selection because they would no longer have to rely so much on higher-yielding equities to meet dividend targets. This would give them a greater freedom as to where to invest. Using capital would also allow greater flexibility for trusts to pay out a stable dividend for a long period of time – and ride out the ups and downs of the economic cycle.

There is a good chance that raising dividends from capital could tighten discounts. In 2011, this was the reason why the activist hedge fund Laxey Partners wanted Alliance Trust to raise its dividends from its capital profits. Higher dividends do tend to narrow if not eliminate discounts – particularly in this low-interest environment. Laxey Partners argued that this would have been a cheaper option for Alliance than share buybacks, and more effective. It may have had a point.

If you look at the range of discounts across the various sectors, there is little doubt that higher-yielding investment trusts are trading on tighter discounts or premiums to NAV compared to lower-dividend payers. Of course, there are exceptions. Lower-yielding trusts with excellent short- and long-term investment records are highly sought, and this is reflected in tight or zero discounts. I can think of Finsbury Growth & Income and

Aberdeen Asian Smaller Companies – neither are high yielders but both consistently close to NAV.

Conversely, high-yielding trusts which have mediocre track records can stand at discounts – although it is noticeable how few exist today. What is more, it is interesting to note that higher-yielding investment trusts have tended to trade on lower discounts over the longer term – this is not just a recent phenomenon because of low interest rates. And this is despite the often better total return performance from their lower-yielding peers.

This perhaps is understandable. There will be a greater demand for an income trust. Those who require income are unlikely to go elsewhere and, as the population ages, this demand will hardly abate. These investors will not tend to look at low or zero dividend trusts. However, in circumstances where income is not the priority, investors are likely to consider all trusts – income or not. It is this group of investors who are rightly interested in achieving good total returns – income and capital growth combined. And they do not mind how this is achieved, whether by capital growth alone or a combination of the two.

This legal change could have a profound impact on the sector.

Enhanced flexibility

In recent years, trusts have acquired greater flexibility when it comes to the financial instruments available for use. This was largely because of the 2011 Finance Act that tidied up much investment trust legislation: for example, it removed the need to seek approval to be an investment trust every year.

But the key changes concerned permitted investments. This included the removal of the 15 per cent maximum holding limit – whereby single holdings were not permitted to exceed 15 per cent of the total value of a portfolio's assets. Holdings can now exceed this level provided this is allowed by the board of directors. Other changes include the creation of a 'white list' of permissible investments within investment trusts and the expansion of the use of derivatives.

The changes will particularly benefit trusts investing in the more exotic asset classes. Most of the new launches during the past decade have been in 'alternatives', such as funds of funds and private hedge funds, and the enhanced flexibility introduced by these rule changes has best suited these types of trusts.

5

Useful investing miscellany

There are some other useful terms and factors that we should cover. Taken together, they can help to inform and thereby increase the chances of getting investment decisions right.

Directors' and managers' shareholdings

As with any public company, it is reassuring for investors to see that those closest to the investment trust have a stake in the company. The larger the stake the better: the interests of investors and those running the trust are more closely aligned. So potential investors should look in the report and accounts, where directors' shareholdings are listed, and ascertain whether these directors increased or decreased their stakes over the year.

The actions of fund managers – and not just their warm words – are also worth noting when it comes to shareholdings. Most fund managers can talk a convincing story about the merits of their particular trust – and regularly do so when making presentations to existing and potential investors. Many are well paid. Yet too few have a decent shareholding, or indeed any stake at all.

It is no coincidence that those trusts that do have fund managers with decent stakes tend to perform well. For example, Alex Darwell has for some time had a significant shareholding in the Jupiter European Opportunities

Investment Trust (JEO) which he runs together with its mirror unit trust. Both have a phenomenal track record against both the benchmark and peers – but it is the investment trust that shines the most.

Monitoring fund managers' holdings can also give reassurance in other areas. Sometimes fund managers change – it is the way of things. Some are replaced because of poor performance. Some move on through their own volition. When the latter happens it is worth keeping an eye on shareholdings. It is also interesting to note whether positive noises from the fund manager about future prospects, particularly if supported by higher gearing, is matched by that manager or director adding to their holdings.

For example, I know of one investment trust where the report and accounts state that the fund manager responsible for its excellent per-formance has stood aside, whilst still running other funds on behalf of the group he founded and built. The report reassures readers that this manager will still provide 'guidance and strategic oversight'. What it could have highlighted better is that the manager in question retains a £2 million stake in the trust – now that is reassuring!

The report and accounts

I have mentioned the report and accounts a number of times, and investors are recommended to obtain a copy of the trust's accounts before dealing. These can usually be printed from the trust's website, but if hard copies are required then the website will give contact details, and most companies oblige promptly. There is the main annual report and accounts, but also an update at the half-year stage. Most trusts also produce useful monthly factsheets which are available from their websites.

These publications remind the investor of the benchmark and invest-ment objective and policy. The benchmark is usually a single index such as the FTSE All-Share, but can be a combination of indices perhaps reflecting the generalist nature of the trust. Murray International Trust (MYI), which is a holding in my Income portfolio, has a composite index made up of 40 per cent of the FTSE World UK index and 60 per cent of the FTSE World ex-UK index. Being benchmark aware is important, particularly when comparing the performances of different trusts. There is little point in comparing trusts' performance if they have different benchmarks.

The performance and investment highlights are also covered, together with other useful information such as the level of discount over the year and the extent of any share buybacks. The chairman's statement comments on such things as investment performance, dividend payments, any board changes and share buybacks. Typically, the statement will take a general view by putting into context the portfolio's performance relative to the bigger economic and market picture – usually worth a read.

The fund managers' report is also worth reading. This covers the portfolio's performance in some detail. It will usually describe how the past year (or half year) has unfolded, the rationale behind portfolio changes, and the contribution to performance from different sections of the portfolio. A list of best and worst performers is included, as is a complete list of the portfolio's holdings and also usually a paragraph or two about the top 10 or 20 holdings. Pie charts will detail portfolio breakdown by sector, geography (if there is an overseas component) and sometimes by market capitalisation. The reader is left in no doubt as to the portfolio's recent history and present state.

However, the future is more important than the past. The manager's report will usually look forward and give the reader a useful insight into future strategy and outlook – something which is not usually well covered in the monthly factsheets. It will focus on how the portfolio is positioned relative to the manager's assessment of the economic situation. This is the most interesting part of the report, particularly when the manager in question has a good track record. It will also indicate the extent of any changes to the gearing of the trust. Adding to gearing usually reflects a positive outlook, and vice versa.

The report and accounts will also detail information about the directors, their remuneration, shareholdings, board attendance record and any changes. The trust after all belongs to its shareholders. There is then the directors' report and financial statements which will hopefully prove that the accountants believe the books balance. Bringing up the rear is usually a glossary of terms, corporate information and general shareholder information including contact details.

Doing the splits

Split capital investment trusts (splits) are like ordinary trusts in that they have a portfolio of investments which are managed on behalf of shareholders. However, splits issue more than one class of equity share – unlike conventional trusts which issue just the one. These different shares have different pre-determined entitlements to the capital and income returns of the portfolio. At least one component will have a fixed wind-up date – if not all.

This sounds complex, but is not. A normal investment trust will have equal ranking shares with the same entitlement to capital growth (or loss) plus any dividends along the way. In its simplest form, a split will have two types of share. An income share will entitle the shareholder to all the dividends generated by the underlying portfolio during its life, plus perhaps a predetermined capital value as well on wind-up. A capital share will entitle access to the remaining capital value of the portfolio upon wind-up, once any income share entitlements to capital value have been honoured.

This allows shareholders with different priorities to pursue different strategies from the same portfolio. Elderly investors might appreciate the income, whilst younger investors may favour the capital shares. There is a predetermined order of entitlement to the portfolio both during its life and at wind-up, which should also take into account other prior charges such as loans.

There is typically a third type of share called a zero-dividend preference share (a zero for short). As the name implies, no dividends are paid but the share is worth a certain predetermined value at wind-up if the portfolio has enough assets to sustain the entitlement. For example, you buy a zero at 70p and when the trust is wound-up in four years' time it will be worth 100p provided there are sufficient assets. No income is paid along the way. Meanwhile, like all share classes, it can be traded in the markets.

Being a fixed return, the attractions of such a return will vary according to the outlook for interest rates. If interest rates look set to shoot upwards, then the relative attractions of holding the zero look far less, and vice versa. The fact it has a fixed return also distinguishes it from the capital share, which will normally have entitlement to the remaining capital – whatever that may be – once the zero and income shares have been satisfied upon wind-up. The predetermined order of entitlement at wind-up is therefore zeros, income and then capital shares.

Let me give you a real example of a split that will better illustrate the aspects of these different shares.

Example

The M&G High Income Investment Trust runs a portfolio consisting mostly of UK equities with a small balance in corporate bonds. Overall, the portfolio's yield is around 3.8% at the time of writing. The fund manager has beaten the UK FTSE All-Share index since inception. The trust is due to wind up on 17 March 2017 and its present NAV per share is around 150p.

There are three classes of share – zeros, income and capital. The share capital of the trust was split into three equal numbers of shares, equating to 250 million shares each.

The holders of the zeros are entitled to the first 122.83224p per share upon wind-up, or lesser sum as remains, of the final assets of the trust (see Figure 5.1). They are first in the queue for the assets that are available on wind-up. At the time of writing, they can be bought for 98p. This represents an annual return of around 5 per cent over the next four years, which, if held in an ISA or crystallised within your capital gains tax (CGT) exemption, would be tax-free as these shares represent a capital return. You would need to keep an eye on portfolio performance: the zeros are well covered at the moment (NAV is 150p), but a market setback of 15–20 per cent would change the risk profile. However, on balance they would appear to represent good value assuming interest rates remain low for the next few years.

	1st	2nd	3rd
Start of the queue	Zeros: first 122.83p of assets	Income shares: next 70p of assets	Capital: anything left over

Figure 5.1 The various entitlements of the three classes of share of the M&G High Income Investment Trust

Meanwhile, the income shares (MGHi) are entitled to the next 70p per share subject to the prior entitlement of the zeros. With the number of shares being equally split three ways, all the dividends paid are channelled into just a third of the shares, which means the running yield of these income shares is around 11%. This is attractive but remember the present NAV is around 150p, and so their present 'capital' worth is 27p (150p NAV – 122.83p zero entitlement). The income shares are presently priced at 47p. Given the running yield, I consider these attractive despite the projected capital loss – something which could change if markets advance – which is why my Investors Chronicle Income portfolio holds them.

Finally, capital shareholders will be paid the balance of net assets on wind-up after the prior zero and income entitlements have been met in full. By their very nature, these are the riskiest of the three shares: no investor knows how well the portfolio and markets will perform up to 2017. They are entitled to all assets exceeding 193p (122.83p zero entitlement + 70p income entitlement) – 43p ahead of where the NAV presently stands. If markets do well, they could be a good investment with a price today of 4p.

In short, splits are complex and require continual monitoring. I have introduced them here so readers can get a flavour and ask the right questions when necessary. Investors need to fully understand the capital structure, the order of entitlements and the underlying portfolio before investing. I suggest you seek professional advice, unless you fully understand the various factors at play.

ETFs and trackers

You may have heard a lot about exchange-traded funds or ETFs. They are simply collective investment funds (like investment or unit trusts) that aim to track or mirror the performance of a particular market – whether it is a sector, entire equity or bond index, commodity or currency. They are listed on a stock exchange and are open-ended like unit trusts and OEICs and so investors can buy or redeem units.

One of the key attractions of EFTs is that they charge low fees. Being a tracker or 'passive' fund there is no expensive fund management team trying to beat the market – to be 'active' managers. This saving is passed on to shareholders. Most ETFs have a total expense ratio (TER) well below 1 per cent and sometimes as low as 0.2 per cent for bond funds. As highlighted in previous chapters, this compares with an average TER of 1.6 per cent for actively managed unit trusts, and this does not include the 'hidden' costs of dealing which can often push the real expense ratio towards 2.5 per cent and more.

ETFs have proved to be an attractive proposition for essentially two reasons. The first is that investors are becoming increasingly aware that most active managers underperform. Various studies show that as much 90 per cent of such managers have failed to beat their index over three years. So why pay up for such service? Why not just track the market with a low-cost ETF that does what it says?

The second reason is that in this low-growth environment where equity markets are expected to make pedestrian progress at best, cost-effective investing becomes more attractive. Previous chapters have illustrated the extent to which higher fees can eat into performance over the longer term. So again, why pay up – particularly when more and more ETFs are coming to market offering even more choice to investors?

I happen to disagree with both propositions. Particularly when it comes to investment trusts, there is no shortage of good, active, fund managers who outperform their benchmarks. Certainly enough to justify the construction of an investment trust portfolio – but I would say that wouldn't I! There is then the issue of tracking itself. Because of the fees charged, low though they may be, and tracking error which usually proves a negative, by their very nature ETFs will underperform the markets they promise to mirror. It is a fact of life.

However, my considerations aside, I can understand why ETFs have grown enormously in popularity. They were first introduced in the US in 1993 and have been around in Europe for over 12 years. But they have enjoyed exponential growth and this will continue. A 2011 survey from Charles Schwab[1] suggested that nearly half of their investors were planning to increase their ETF holdings.

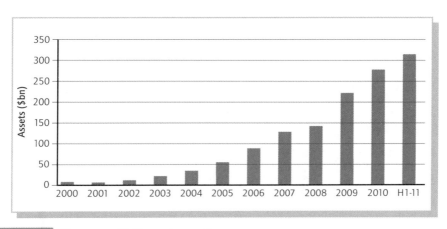

Figure 5.2   European ETF asset growth

Source: From Barnes, D. (2011), 'Synthetic appeal', *Securities and Investment Review*, October.

Lower fees to one side, ETFs have a number of other attractions. They do not usually trade at wide discounts to NAV as investment trusts can. ETFs give investors quick access to a market in one trade, and allow smaller investors easier access to hitherto forbidden investments such as gold and oil – assets that are less correlated to mainstream securities such as shares and bonds. ETFs also cover a wider range of assets compared to the few unit trust trackers that exist, including those less liquid ones. It is interesting to note that when some corporate bond markets froze in 2008–09, credit bond ETFs by and large kept trading. Furthermore, ETFs can be traded at will whereas other trackers can only be traded once a day and are more expensive.

For a combination of these advantages, I do have a few ETFs in both my *Investors Chronicle* investment trust portfolios. Typically they are there to gain exposure to bond markets, for this is an area not well covered by investment trusts. I also use ETFs when it comes to boosting income from emerging markets and when wanting to gain exposure to the gold price. Again, areas not well covered or not covered at all. All these EFTs have contributed to performance.

But investors should also be aware of the risks and other characteristics of ETFs before investing. ETFs can be divided into physical and swap-based or 'synthetic'. Physical ETFs own at least a selection of the assets in the index they are tracking – a FTSE 100 ETF will physically own some if not all of the individual companies. By comparison, a synthetic ETF relies on a third-party investment bank to provide the index return via an index swap contract with that bank, which is designed to duplicate the performance of the index in question.

Investors in synthetic ETFs must therefore be aware that there is always a third party solvency risk, no matter how small. If that third party were to fail and go bust, then there is every chance you would not get back much of your money. In Europe, counterparty risk is limited to 10%, which is therefore the maximum an investor would lose.

But there is also a counterparty risk for holders of physical ETFs when these ETFs lend stocks to a third party – they may not, in extreme cases, be able to get them back. However, we should remember that actively managed funds such as unit trusts also engage in stock lending.

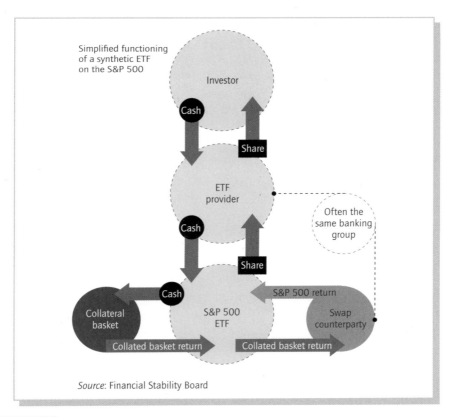

Simplified functioning
of a synthetic ETF
on the S&P 500

Investor

Cash

Share

ETF
provider

Often the
same banking
group

Cash

Share

Cash

S&P 500 return

Collateral
basket

S&P 500
ETF

Swap
counterparty

Collated basket return

Collated basket return

Source: Financial Stability Board

Figure 5.3   **How do synthetic ETFs work?**

I have touched on an ETF's tracking error earlier, but it is worthy of note. Rarely does an ETF exactly duplicate its index. This can happen for a number of reasons, but common among them is the fact that an ETF often only buys a sample of the index rather than all of its components. This happens more in smaller company markets when it is difficult to hold all stocks in what can be illiquid markets. Tracking errors rarely favour the investor and, when added to the ETF's charges, result in a performance marginally lagging behind the index in question.

But even tracking a mainstream index such as the FTSE 100, different ETF providers can have quite different tracking errors. Looking at the tracking difference between providers over two years, the figure varies from around 0.5 per cent behind the index through to 2.0 per cent behind the index. As we have seen in earlier chapters, these 'small' figures become large ones over time. Typically, the ETF's TER can account for around half the figure. So investors beware! In fairness to the ETF industry, serious attempts are being made to reduce these tracking errors – a challenge given added impetus by their ever-increasing popularity.

Finally, you should also be aware that some leveraged ETFs borrow money to amplify returns, and some aim to provide the inverse daily performance of the index. Complicated stuff, so investors should seek advice.

Portfolio turnover

Investors should be aware of the extent to which their fund managers are 'turning over' the underlying portfolio. The former, and much maligned, US president Ronald Reagan was once reputed to have said: 'Don't just stand there, do nothing.' It is sound advice for investors and fund managers alike.

A study by FE Trustnet in 2011[2] revealed that fund managers with a high portfolio turnover underperform those who do not change their holdings as frequently. The research group compared performance between the 10 per cent of unit trusts with the highest and lowest turnover over one year. To confirm the robustness of their findings, they sampled across three fund styles – balanced managed, actively managed, and cautiously balanced. It is no surprise that, on average, returns were 0.8 per cent lower per year for those 10 per cent of funds with the highest turnover. Investors will be aware of the extent to which this small figure can have a detrimental effect on portfolio performance over the years.

The reason is easy to understand. High turnover results in high dealing costs, which of course eat into performance returns. And these dealing costs are not transparent – in many respects they are hidden. Dealing costs, including brokerage fees and stamp duty, are not included in the various measures gauging expense ratios, including the TER. Yet given that each trade can cost around 1 per cent, they can have a significant impact on total costs. Some estimates suggest excessive turnover can add as much as 0.8–0.9 per cent to the TER – which ostensibly comes in at only 1.6 per cent. Such figures tally with FE Trustnet's findings.

The worrying development for investors is that turnover is on the increase. FE Trustnet has pointed out that the average period for holding a stock is around nine months, whereas 50 years ago it was around eight years. Part of the reason is a short-term culture among fund managers encouraged by an institutional adherence to benchmarks and a remuneration policy to match – something we will cover in future chapters. But it also has to be said that some investors are partly to blame: their short-term focus also encourages fund managers to deliver positive returns and news in the short term.

This is where investment trusts have an advantage. These managers do not have to worry about money flows. Because investors trade the shares, which does not impact on money flowing in and out of the underlying portfolio, the manager has the luxury of taking a long-term approach to investing. As such, dealing costs tend to be lower.

As if to highlight this point, it is interesting to note that a disproportionate number of the trust managers who have excellent long-term track records do tend to keep dealing to a minimum. This is not a coincidence. Nick Train runs one of the trusts in my Growth portfolio called Finsbury Growth & Income (FGT). It has performed superbly over the years. Part of his investment philosophy is to hold shares for the long-term regardless of short-term volatility, with the aim of doubling their value and more. This makes for extremely low portfolio turnover and dealing costs, so helping performance.

Indeed, because it is not easy for investors to track the impact of dealing costs on performance – little data are published – choosing fund managers with a 'long-term' investing style is a sound approach. Another such manager is the well-respected Neil Woodford at Invesco Perpetual. He has an average holding period of five years, which has served both him and investors well in the past.

Different investment styles

Finally, allied to fund managers' varied approach to portfolio turnover, investors also should be aware that there are a number of different investment styles used by different managers. This is important to understand if only because a portfolio slanted towards one particular style may be taking on more risk than was generally assumed. The fund's website will usually give an indication, and the report and accounts certainly will.

But recognising different styles also helps in other respects. It assists in understanding why certain investments do better than others when there is a change in stock market direction or leadership, for 'seeing through' fund managers' poor performance over the short term, and for monitoring progress towards achieving investment objectives.

It is worth remembering from earlier chapters that most 'active' fund managers underperform the market. Chapter 2 highlighted that in the majority of investment sectors the average actively managed unit trust has underperformed its benchmark index over the past 10 years – sometimes by a wide margin.

Indeed, in every sector there were periods lasting some years when the index beat the sector average. Investors would have done better in cheaper passive funds such as ETFs. However, the research also rightly confirmed that some active managers do consistently outperform. The challenge is to identify them.

Having done so, it is wise to understand investment styles. If an investor is seeking a decent and growing income then typically they will be drawn to a portfolio consisting of good quality blue-chip companies. Many will be considered 'defensive' in that they are able to grow earnings, and hence dividends, better than most through the various economic cycles. Such sectors include pharmaceuticals, utilities and household goods. These sectors typically do well when economic growth is sluggish.

This is less the case when economic growth is picking up, for here more 'cyclical' companies – usually yielding less – are deemed to benefit better from the healthier economic climate. Sectors include banking, construction, technology and smaller companies in general.

Meanwhile, some fund managers and trusts can be categorised as having a 'value' or 'growth' bias. Value managers will typically be looking to invest in undervalued companies in a recovery or turnaround phase, and which may be standing at a significant discount to assets if broken up and sold. A growth manager will focus on those companies that consistently generate above-average earnings growth, and perhaps are cheap relative to the market given the extent of growth. Again, the prospects for both types of companies will be influenced by the prevailing economic cycle.

Appreciating the investment style of the manager can help investors see through difficult periods. If a manager sticks with one particular style but is not performing well relative to the market in the short term, it could be because of the economic cycle. This does not make him or her a bad manager: it may simply be because the individual's investment style is out of favour. This raises once again the importance of looking at longer-term performance.

The legendary investor Anthony Bolton is a good case in point. His track record when running the Fidelity UK Special Situations fund was superb – it was beyond comparison. However, he then agreed to come out of a brief retirement to run the freshly launched Fidelity China Special Situations investment trust just months before the Chinese market crashed in 2011. The NAV collapsed 32 per cent during the year, well beyond the benchmark fall of 17 per cent. But the underperformance was not because Bolton had suddenly become a bad manager, but rather because his 'value' style of investing meant he was more exposed during the downturn. I would hope for better performance as the economy recovers.

The well-respected Neil Woodford is another example. He very much believes in investing in blue-chip companies with predictable earnings and good dividends – the 'defensives' which usually do well in a tough economic environment. But these types of companies do not do so well when there is a strong economic recovery. Accordingly, there have been periods – sometimes lasting a few years – when he has trailed the market. But he has stuck to his guns, and come through.

Understanding the investment style of your fund manager is therefore crucially important. Do not be eased out of a good fund through ignorance. But it is also important to ensure your fund managers are indeed sticking to their guns, and not being whip-lashed by markets. Be wary of managers who chop and change their style, perhaps trying to keep up with markets, unless they have a proven track record. You should always be careful of labelling managers too easily, but such factors need to be considered when investing.

I will finish this chapter by mentioning momentum investing. This is when shares that have already been performing well are bought, and when poor performing shares are sold.

A recent report by Credit Suisse and the London Business School (LBS)[3] suggests that the momentum approach would have produced much higher long-term returns than passive or index-tracking, value investing or smaller companies. Figures show that, since 1900, buying the previous year's top performing shares would have produced annualised returns of 14.3 per cent in the UK – compared to just 9.5 per cent for the market. Similar results occurred in most of the other developed markets.

The success of this approach is possibly explained by share prices taking time to reflect new information. However, this winning strategy can produce volatile results and has been known to disappoint when markets suddenly change direction. In 2009, when markets bounced strongly following the credit crisis, momentum investing would have missed the start of the recovery and missed those shares, such as banks, which had been falling but then bounced the most.

Once again it shows, and it deserves repeating, that investment styles do not necessarily work every year and can, indeed, be out of fashion for many years. But what the track record of momentum investing also seems to confirm is the old adage that, if change is thought necessary or cash needed, it is usually better to sell your losers and stick with the winners.

6

Deciding investment objectives

In earlier chapters we looked at investment trusts in some detail and compared them to their competition. The conclusion has been positive: they are a better investment vehicle for the long-term investor. We have also looked at other factors that should be considered, including the different investment styles of fund managers.

But, as an investor, how do you put this theory into practice? Whether monitoring how others run your portfolio, or doing it yourself, how should a portfolio be constructed and managed? These questions will be answered in the next three chapters. But first, the starting point in any investment journey is deciding your investment objectives.

Saving and investing

The very first question to ask is whether you should be investing in the market at all, because there is a difference between saving and investing. Most people are saving for something – whether it is a car, kitchen or holiday. These are short-term objectives and the answer is to put cash aside in a building society or bank until the target has been reached. Certainty counts for a lot.

Other short-term objectives for your cash should be to provide sufficient life insurance for any children and other dependants, the establishment and maintenance of a will if sufficient assets justify this, and the elimination of any costly debt such as credit cards or loans. I would also suggest surplus cash be used to put any mortgages on a capital repayment basis.

That said, most people will also be planning for the longer term. Such plans could be for the children's education, retirement or some long-promised special treat. This takes more thought. Because of the timescale involved you need to be aware of the effects or ravages of inflation. Assuming inflation at 2 per cent, £10,000 today will be worth just £8,000 in 10 years' time. As it happens, inflation is higher at the moment and some believe it could rise further.

This means that, in order to finance your long-term plans, you need to invest your money in something that will grow faster than it would in a bank account. Some people choose any number of assets, for example property, gold, art and wine. But these usually require expertise if not decent deposits. For most people, particularly those starting with relatively modest sums, the answer is the stock market.

Risk tolerances: time and volatility

However, like other assets such as property and gold, investing in bonds and equities involves taking on risk. Prices can fall, and sometimes dramatically. You can lose some or all of your money depending on the nature of your investments. So your starting point is to gauge your risk tolerances – to know how comfortable you feel when investing in the stock market even when your portfolio is falling in price.

Generally speaking, high returns mean high risk. There are no free lunches. The greater the potential for return, the greater the chance of suffering a loss. If it were any other way, then more investors would be focused on riskier investments and doing very well. But it does not work like that. The stock market mirrors life generally – the riskier activities involve more potential downside!

And this is particularly the case for equities. Government or corporate debt – known as bonds – tends to be less risky than equities because performance is less dependent on the company's short-term profits. Debt interest tends to get paid regardless of short-term swings in profitability.

However, at the extremes, this rule can break down. High-risk debt can eclipse solid blue-chip equities when it comes to losses – as holders of Greek government bonds have recently discovered. But as a general rule, bonds are 'safer' – they are less volatile and less risky.

So, with this in mind, what factors should influence your risk tolerances? The greatest risk, apart from perhaps the opportunity cost of investing, is that of losing money. I suggest the two key factors are your time horizons and the extent to which you can tolerate volatility in the value of your investments.

Time horizons

You should only invest in the stock market if you have a decent time horizon. All the evidence shows that equities, with dividends re-invested, perform better than bonds or cash in a bank over the longer term. Figures produced in the annual Credit Suisse Global Investment Returns Yearbook are revealing. Looking back since 1900, global equities have returned an annual 5 per cent after inflation, compared to 1.8 per cent for bonds and 0.9 per cent for cash. In the UK, the respective figures are 5.2 per cent, 1.5 per cent and 0.9 per cent.[1]

Logic dictates that good companies should be growing profits faster than prevailing interest rates. Otherwise, what is the point of being in business: entrepreneurs might just as well put their money in the bank and avoid risk?

Shareholders in such companies should benefit accordingly, but the path is rarely a smooth one. Equity investors can suffer poor decades. Factors such as economic cycles, management decisions and often luck ensure share prices fluctuate more in value than cash earning interest in the bank and provide lacklustre returns. Therefore, the longer an investor can remain invested the better. Financial advisers vary in detailing what 'longer term' actually means, but I suggest a minimum of five to ten years is required when it comes to equities.

There used to be a very approximate guide that the percentage of bonds in a portfolio should reflect the investor's age – for example, 30 per cent if aged 30 and so on. This reflected the view that as an investor got older and time horizons shorter, they would want to reduce the risk of the portfolio by investing in bonds. This would particularly be the case as you came closer to meeting the funding objective, in order to reduce the risk of a short-term fall in the portfolio's value scuppering the looming requirement.

Volatility

The second factor affecting your risk appetite will be how sensitive you are to market volatility. If the thought of a significant drop in the value of your investments – even if only over the short term – worries you then perhaps you need to reduce your investment risk. There is little point in owning an investment portfolio if it keeps you up at night – it is not good for your health. The money would be better placed in a bank or spent on making people happy.

Reducing investment risk can essentially be done in two ways. You can reduce the risk profile within the portfolio by increasing the proportion of bonds and cash relative to equities. Or you can reduce the size of the portfolio itself and put the cash in the bank. But this of course then increases another risk, and that is not being able to fund your longer term goals because money is lacking. There is always an opportunity cost to investing. If your money is placed in low-risk, low-return assets then you risk missing higher returns generated elsewhere. You also risk inflation eroding your wealth over time.

Finally, whether monitoring your financial adviser or running your own portfolio, it is important that regular checks are made to ensure that the risk profiles of both client and portfolio are aligned. In 2011, the Financial Services Authority (FSA) conducted a regulatory investigation into 16 wealth managers. It found that the majority had failed to match the level of risk with the objectives or circumstances of the investor.

Further research by the FT into wealth managers found many balanced portfolios held significant levels of equities – at one firm, 83 per cent of client money in a 'balanced' portfolio was invested in shares.[2] Poor record keeping was thought to be the cause, rather than mis-selling. But the episode does illustrate the need to check that risk profiles match.

Currency considerations

Most UK investors will think in sterling because their assets and liabilities are based in the UK. Accordingly, they tend to have the majority of their portfolio invested in the UK. But some investors may have assets or liabilities based abroad, and may consequently want to hedge their currency risk – so not to lose money because of currency swings – by having portfolio exposure in that particular country or currency.

This can be done by investing in equities, bonds or indeed cash denominated accordingly in the chosen currency, or by investing in funds specialising in the country where the currency exposure is not hedged. Such considerations can often influence investment weightings within a portfolio.

But investors may also think other currencies are attractive as an investment in their own right, and want to benefit accordingly within their portfolios. As such, it is always worth investigating whether an investment trust is hedged or not – because this can have a big impact on portfolio returns.

If un-hedged then, regardless of how well the underlying portfolio performs relative to its own index or stock market, its total value will be influenced by swings in the local currency relative to the pound. A 10 per cent gain in the portfolio will be lost if the local currency weakens by more than 10 per cent against the pound. But it can also work the other way. A local currency, in whose market a portfolio is invested, which strengthens against the pound can enhance the returns gained from that portfolio.

By contrast, a hedged portfolio is, by and large, not influenced by currency moves because the fund manager has 'pegged' the local currency to sterling via the derivatives market. Swings in the portfolio's currency will not affect the total value when it is transferred back into sterling. In one respect, this reduces risk, for currencies are notoriously difficult to predict, particularly in the short term.

The key reason for this is that politicians, including the central bankers appointed by them, are an additional factor – over and above economics

– that can disproportionately influence matters. And politics can add an unpredictable mix to the economic equation. For example, if economics was left to prevail, the euro would have fractured by now – with countries like Greece having defaulted and left the single currency. But the single currency has a political dimension – that of 'ever closer political union', as described in the Treaty of Rome. Therefore, economics takes a back seat to a very large extent.

I prefer to look at the longer-term factors that influence currencies, and which usually prove the more powerful. Strong currencies are typically the hallmark of countries with strong finances, a positive balance of trade and sound politics: one reason being that these countries do not usually have to buy other currencies, and therefore sell their own, to fund debt or trade deficits. Whatever the meddling of politicians or central bankers, the realities of the market usually prevail.

It is no coincidence that a number of Asian countries enjoy strong currencies compared with their more indebted counterparts in the West. Investors can benefit accordingly by gaining exposure to these currencies, simply by holding their bonds and equities – through funds or individual holdings – ensuring, of course, that their exposure is un-hedged.

It should also be recognised that currency movements can influence stock markets. For example, falls in sterling have usually been good for the UK market. Since 1990 there have been 64 months in which both the pound fell by more than 1 per cent and the FTSE All-Share index rose by an average of 1 per cent. To illustrate that the correlation holds good in all weathers, there have also been 79 months in which the pound rose by more than 1 per cent and the markets fell by an average of 0.6 per cent.

This relationship exists because around 60 per cent of the stock market's earnings are derived from overseas – a falling pound will typically increase the value of overseas earnings. Furthermore, a weaker pound should also help exporters as goods manufactured will be cheaper, and therefore more competitive. Both consequences should boost shares. But whatever the reason, the anticipated direction of sterling may be a factor in determining a UK investor's investment objectives.

Income requirements

Another factor to consider when clarifying your investment objectives is your income requirement. You may be investing in the market because income is important to you and it is difficult finding it elsewhere. Certainly at the moment, with interest rates low and set to remain so, the stock market offers some attractive alternative ways of generating income through mostly bonds and cash. Good corporate bonds and decent yielding blue-chips are certainly in demand by investors.

You may be seeking a growing income in which case good-quality equities should very much feature in your portfolios. As companies grow and prosper, many reward their shareholders with increased dividends. Many companies, including numerous investment trusts, have excellent longer-term track records in growing their dividends – helped by healthy revenue reserves built up over many years. This can be important to investors who have income requirements, and ones that are growing. This is typically the case with elderly investors who have health and care costs or who may wish to help with the costs of grandchildren.

Because interest rates have been so low and look set to remain so for the foreseeable future, good-yielding and decent-quality investment trusts are typically standing at a premium to net assset value (NAV) at the moment. This is not just confined to blue-chip equities but also those trusts that invest in corporate bonds, property, smaller companies, infrastructure etc. – anything that offers a high and sustainable yield.

Investors need to be careful. One of the attractions of trusts is the discount – the idea that you are buying assets at a discount. By paying a premium, it could be argued you are overpaying. And when market shocks come along or sector leadership changes, then a widening discount can compound the loss. But it remains the case that a quality portfolio of trusts can be created which yields well in excess of what banks can offer – and this portfolio would hope to grow dividends over time.

One final thought. It used to be the case that if an investor wanted equity income, then the UK market was where it was found. Overseas equities yielded less in comparison. Income-hungry portfolios would therefore be biased towards the UK. However, this is changing.

For a variety of reasons, more and more overseas companies are becoming dividend payers with a particular emphasis on the Far East and emerging markets generally. Indeed, companies in emerging markets now pay over 40 per cent of the world's equity income. This relatively recent development has important consequences when it comes to asset allocation – investors should take note.

Choosing a benchmark

Having identified your risk tolerances, you can create a portfolio. But how do you know whether the investments chosen to reflect these tolerances are performing well relative to other possible investments? After all, there are usually a range of investments available that could have been chosen to reflect your risk profile. Markets may well swing around, but as an investor you should at least have an indication as to whether these investments have been well chosen. The wiser the choice, the faster you reach those longer-term goals.

This is where benchmarks come in. They are a method of measuring how well the chosen investments are performing once a portfolio has been constructed. The benchmark should reflect the portfolio's objectives and risk profile, to ensure we are comparing apples with apples. But there is a big debate as to what benchmarks to use, and just how relevant they are.

For those investors who simply want a real or absolute return, such as inflation + 1 per cent, or cash + 2 per cent, then the benchmark is straightforward. Risk is therefore minimised, but not eliminated. But for those who want superior returns over the longer term, and are willing to take on a commensurate level of risk, then the issue of benchmarks becomes more important.

When the live portfolios were created for my *Investors Chronicle* column, I chose the Growth and Income indices of the Association of Private Client Investment Managers and Stockbrokers (APCIMS) as the benchmarks to objectively measure how well the portfolios were performing. Performance relative to these benchmarks is updated each month.

These benchmarks are widely recognised. One of their attractions is that the different components of each benchmark are made up of the actual indices – the relevant markets – as illustrated by Figure 6.1. Occasionally, the asset allocations are changed in response to quarterly surveys to ensure the benchmarks continue to reflect investors' requirements.

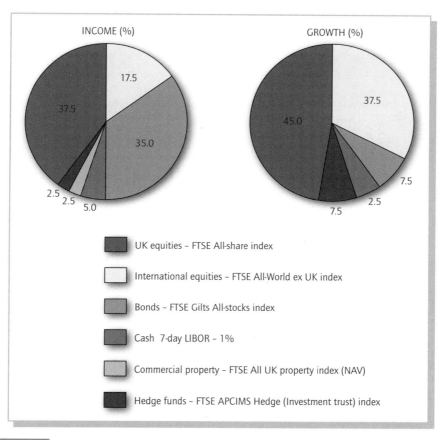

Figure 6.1   FTSE APCIMS Private Investor Index Series Asset Allocation

But such benchmarks will not suit everyone. A client's risk profile and objectives may not match the bond/equity weightings as reflected in either. In my fund management days, I used to regularly agree with clients on a composite benchmark made up from the relevant market indices. Clients then had something to gauge how well the portfolio was performing.

But things have moved on. There are now benchmarks that compare how well a portfolio is performing relative to both its peer group and the amount of risk inherent in the portfolio – in effect, measuring a unit of return against a unit of risk. After all, some equity portfolios are riskier than others. Is it right, for example, that a portfolio biased towards 'defensive' sectors (such as pharmaceuticals, tobacco and food retailers) compared to one biased towards the more economically sensitive sectors (such as mining, technology and banks) should be measured equally against the FTSE All-Share from whence they all come?

Such benchmarks help investors become aware of what are called risk-adjusted returns. But I maintain that for the majority of investors it is wise not to lose sight of how the indices themselves are performing. Otherwise, peer-like comparisons can make for herd-like performance. This is one reason the APCIMS benchmarks are widely recognised.

There are two other points that should be mentioned briefly about benchmarks. Once the portfolio is up and running, it is essential to regularly assess the relevance of the benchmark. Your circumstances and risk profiles change over time, and the benchmarks need to reflect this. This is especially true if performance has deviated from the benchmark by some measure – in which case, both the investments and the benchmark need to be reviewed.

Finally, you should always remember the golden rule about benchmarks: never let them dictate how a portfolio is constructed. They are a method of measuring performance, not a blue-print to copy slavishly. This is important to understand. A weighting in any index tells you about the past in that it reflects how well a particular company or country has performed, relative to its peers. But it says nothing of the future.

The investment objective should be to beat the benchmark, which means you have to deviate from it – and not mimic it. Otherwise, you are simply trading an investment simply because everyone else has – the worst reason to trade and the first step on the road to ruin. You can only beat the benchmark by thinking differently – not by copying it. When it comes to buying investment trusts, focus on those fund managers who have a good track record at being able to do this.

'But the roof extension looked good on that house!'

The route to market

Having considered the factors that help you to determine investment objectives and the role of benchmarks, investors need to appreciate the choice they have in accessing the market and the tools at their disposal. There are several routes to market: whether as a DIY investor, or taking advice, or allowing a manager to run your portfolio, and a number of options in between.

Many people will already have some exposure to the stock market via their company pension schemes. It is always worth reading the literature these schemes send you, which usually includes a report as to how the assets are performing. Meanwhile, recent government pension initiatives should also be considered. But this area of financial planning is complicated, not helped by a myriad of rules and regulations. You should always seek advice from an independent pension adviser as pensions require expertise. However, focusing on this area can save headaches further down the line.

ISAs and SIPPs

Outside these options, the individual savings account (ISA) and the self-invested personal pension (SIPP) are the two main savings vehicles to consider. These are not investments or assets, but rather tax-free 'wrappers' into which your investments are placed. Both shield investments from capital gains tax (CGT) and income tax, which means the underlying assets should grow faster than they otherwise would.

Each tax year, you can put a sum of money into an ISA which can then be invested in the stock market. The 2013–14 total ISA amount is £11,520. The ISA can be self-select – you choose the investments – or managed by the ISA provider. Up to half the amount can be saved in a cash ISA. Any unused allowance does not carry forward into the next tax year. Money can be withdrawn at any point. Parents can open a 'Junior ISA' for their children and invest up to £3,600 in a tax year but the money cannot be accessed until the child is 18.

A SIPP is a bigger 'wrapper'. £50,000 a year can be invested in a wider range of investments although the lifetime allowance is £1.5 million. Another difference is that the tax break comes up front: a £100 pension contribution would cost a 20 per cent taxpayer £80 and a 40 per cent taxpayer £60 – the government pays the difference. Your money is locked away until you are 55, after which you can withdraw 25 per cent tax-free, but the balance must be used to buy an income which will be taxed.

For choice, I prefer ISAs as they are more flexible. But it does depend on your investment goal and time horizon. A SIPP may be preferable for long-term saving objectives such as retirement. The tax relief is generous, particularly for those higher-rate taxpayers who may expect to pay basic rate tax when they retire. For more medium-term objectives like school fees or house purchases, the flexibility offered by ISAs is hard to beat.

IFAs

Apart from ISAs and SIPPs, most investors will be invested in open-ended funds courtesy of their independent financial advisers (IFAs). The introduction to this book outlined the changes brought in by the Retail Distribution Review (RDR), and how this may affect the small investor.

Many major names such as Lloyds, Barclays and HSBC withdrew from the tied-advice market because of the RDR. This, together with those investors being unwilling to pay up front for advice under the new RDR rules, could well lead to a black hole – or advice gap – in the market. And the numbers are not small. A survey by Deloitte in 2012[3] suggested 5.5 million people will stop taking advice. The consequences could be significant: the emphasis could easily change from banks misselling to clients misbuying.

Meanwhile, IFAs are going to see a reduction in their income. The elimination of trailing commissions and higher costs because of FSA requirements will result in the adviser market having to adjust. Some firms may offer a form of simplified advice. Others may move into asset management, and perhaps adopt a 'model portfolio' approach where clients are slotted into one of a range of strategies best suited to their individual needs. Such an approach is far less labour-intensive than the IFA–client relationship, and so will be cheaper than what IFAs will have to charge under the new RDR regime, but it does require focus in the early stages to ensure the right strategy is chosen.

This post-RDR response by the adviser market will typically suit investors with medium-sized portfolios (£100,000 to £200,000). But if you are a smaller investor it is not yet evident where to go for advice. Perhaps the model portfolio approach will be adapted for smaller investors. Certainly, if Deloitte's figures are even close to the mark, a number of firms may see the potential in this market and react accordingly. It will be worth any investor in this situation surveying the field well before deciding from whom they should seek advice.

Wealth managers

For the very wealthy, there is of course a host of wealth managers across the UK who will help you manage your money. These usually have all the financial services at hand either directly or indirectly. Their business is not just about investing, but also tax and financial planning. But their investment service essentially breaks down into three categories.

1 Discretionary management is where the client clarifies their risk tolerances and income requirements, and then allows the wealth manager to get on with the job.

2 Advisory management is when advice is given to the client, who then cracks on.

3 A managed advisory service is a mix between the two, and involves closer involvement of the client with strategy whilst the manager oversees the day-to-day timing decisions.

If starting from scratch, take the time to meet a few managers. Pay particular attention to their breadth of offering, investment style and fee structure. Investors are spoilt for choice. Personal chemistry is important and, to get the best out of them, they will need to get to know you well – the extent of your wealth, your family circumstances, your goals and time horizons. This person could be advising you for many years so take time in assessing your choices.

An important part of this is the fee and charges structure. Good wealth managers understandably do not come cheap. Many are adapting to the new focus on costs. Some are now charging low initial fees but introducing performance fees. This should be welcomed, but I would ask for fee rebates or credits carried forward should they underperform! But have a clear understanding of costs, so that the early meetings are focused on establishing the portfolio and building trust.

Given the costs, particularly the charges when first establishing a portfolio, I suggest wealth managers are best suited to those investors with a minimum of £150,000 to £200,000 to invest. Much less and they are unlikely to offer value for money. Some well-established names have much higher thresholds: Coutts has recently raised its minimum from £500,000 to £1 million.

Do-it-yourself

Finally, in discussing how best to access markets, never underestimate your own skill!

The *Wall Street Journal* looked at the investment returns generated by retired investors between 1999 and 2009. It compared the performance of those who ran their own portfolios to those who hired a stockbroker. The former group outperformed the latter by around 1.5 per cent a year – amounting to over 16 per cent for the period. Fees accounted for only half the difference.

Very few managers consistently generate 'alpha' – this being the return produced by the manager in excess of the market, having taken into account the risk profile adopted. Instead, investors often receive high fees and mediocre performance. So consider becoming a DIY investor.

Such an investor would need to establish an execution-only service with one of any number of banks or broking firms – they usually advertise their services in the financial press. Dealing online is usually cheaper than the telephone, but check costs – some online trades come in as little as £5 regardless of the size of deal.

Some firms in addition offer model portfolios, research facilities and online tools to help investors make informed decisions – but the decision remains with the investor. Furthermore, there is a welter of advice offered by various websites. With the fixed costs of running a web-based service falling, many advisers are using the internet to service clients both large and small. The range of product varies, including both 'active' and 'passive' or index-tracking options.

My *Investors Chronicle* investment trust portfolios are designed to help the DIY investor. This monthly column sets out two portfolios – one Growth, one Income – and aims to explain the thinking behind any changes to holdings that have occurred during the previous month. Both portfolios are measured against appropriate benchmarks so readers can gauge performance. Being live portfolios, a DIY investor could mirror either or both of these portfolios using an execution-only service. (There is more on these portfolios in Chapter 9).

7

Successful investing

So you have thought through various points and decided upon your investment objectives. You have also decided on whether to be a DIY investor, seek advice or allow a wealth manager to run the portfolio for you. Whatever the chosen method of accessing the stock market, it is important to understand the principles of successful investing so that you can either execute them yourself or be better informed when questioning your adviser or manager. The right knowledge is worth its weight in gold when it comes to investing!

Getting started

Let us start with an investor who, for whatever reason, is sitting on a cash pile that needs to be invested. How do you best construct a portfolio? Theory is fine, but the practice is often more difficult.

If you already have an established portfolio, maybe inherited or taken back from a financial adviser, then this question is less relevant. You can sell your holdings and reinvest the proceeds in investments that better reflect your objectives. In doing so, it is wise to keep an eye on the extent of gains in order to be aware of when you are approaching the annual capital gains tax limit, which for the 2013/14 tax year is £10,600. Any gains beyond this will be taxed at the investor's marginal rate of tax.

Selling should not be a deterrent if you feel that instigating changes would benefit the portfolio. Taxation should not dictate investment policy. However, the CGT limit can influence the timing of changes. This is particularly the case if you are contemplating changes close to the tax year end, in which case two annual exemptions can be utilised by staggering changes into the next tax year. Also remember that portfolios held in joint names will enjoy twice the annual limit.

However, those investors starting from cash have more difficult decisions to make. How quickly should you invest the cash, which investments to start with, how should the cash be best managed until it is invested? You are not alone in contemplating these choices: novice and professional investors toy with such questions. On a number of occasions when working in the City, entrepreneurs asked me to invest a sizeable chunk of the proceeds of a business sale built up over decades, often amounting to several millions of pounds. No matter how confident about the prospects, I was always mindful that a stock market crash could, overnight, wipe out years of work.

The answer in such situations is usually to invest gradually over a period, typically of 6–12 months, trying to buy on bad days. However, you need to be flexible. If there is a market correction, then a more aggressive stance is warranted. A strong run by the market would suggest more caution, at least in the short term. The important thing for me was to have discussed matters with the client so that we were both happy with the strategy. Sometimes clients had strong preferences, which it was usually wise to accommodate, provided they were aware of my assessment.

A similar strategy should be employed by investors creating a portfolio from cash. Money should be invested gradually. There is a term called pound-cost averaging, which describes a version of this tactic. The idea is that an investor should determine to invest an equal amount of cash at regular intervals. This would mean that fewer shares would be bought if the market had had a strong run and prices were high. Conversely, it would also mean more shares would be bought for the same amount of cash if the market had fallen back. Investing at regular intervals has the advantage of taking subjective decisions as to the timing of purchases out of the equation.

On first inspection, the maths looks attractive.

Example

Let's imagine you invest £4,000 at a rate of £1,000 for each of the subsequent four months. Purchase details are as follows:

■ 50 shares are bought at £20 each.

■ The price then falls in month two, so 100 shares are bought at £10 each.

■ 200 shares are bought for £5.

■ Finally, 50 shares are bought again for £20.

In total, 400 shares have been bought for an average cost of £10 (£4,000 divided by 400). By contrast, the average monthly price per share on each of the days of purchase was £13.75 (£20 + £10 + £5 + £20 divided by four). So pound-cost averaging has worked on this occasion.

But pound-cost averaging does not work all the time. The above example takes advantage of a falling share price. But share prices rise more than they fall. During the past 80 years or so, the US market had risen 70 per cent of the time. The market usually outperforms cash. Therefore, there is a good case for lump-sum investing – committing the cash to the market in one go. After all, history is on your side, and it would save on dealing costs.

This message was reinforced by investment consultant Michael Edesess a few years ago. He showed that, over the preceding 83 years, investing a lump sum actually beat investing through pound-cost averaging by more than 3 per cent a year whether you took one-, three- or five-year rolling periods.[1]

Which method is chosen will depend on your attitude to risk. Given that various studies show most investors fear losses more than they hope for gains, then perhaps pound-cost averaging should be seen as an element of insurance against market losses. But given that markets tend to rise rather than fall, it is advisable not to delay completion of the process for too long: the longer it takes, the higher the cost will be. Four to six months feels about right.

And always remember, as an investor you should only be committing to the stock market the proportion of your wealth that allows you to sleep at night even when markets are turbulent. If you cannot do this, then perhaps you should not be invested at all. If low risk is your stated objective, then a bank account is the better option.

Why it is important to stay invested

When committing cash to the market, it is important to try and get timing right. But over the longer term, a more important contribution to successful investing is to stay invested once committed.

Markets are naturally volatile. Much wiser investors than I often take advantage of these short-term market swings and make a lot of money in the process by, for example, selling stocks when they look pricey, and buying them when they are cheaper. This is not investing, it is trading. But a few managers are consistently good at it, and such expertise is highly valued.

However, for the majority of investors, the lessons of history suggest it is better to stay invested. A study carried out by Barclays Wealth in 2010[2] suggested that UK investors were losing on average just over 1 per cent a year because of market timing errors. This does not sound much, but over long periods it can add up. Indeed, Barclays highlighted that in the period 1992–2009, investors who tried to time the market were down 20 per cent compared to those who had simply stuck with it.

The study also suggested that the more volatile the markets, the greater the loss. Investors dealing in global equity funds apparently lost 2.25 per cent a year on average, compared to just losing 0.5 per cent for UK funds. The explanation being that global markets tend to be more volatile, and therefore there was more scope to get market timing wrong – which investors apparently did!

Research from Fidelity[3] seems to reinforce the wisdom of sticking with markets. Fidelity has highlighted the extent to which returns are affected if just a few of the best days are missed. Investors who put £1,000 into the FTSE All-Share in October 2000 would have seen it grow to £1,330 by October 2010 – this was not a good decade by historical standards! But if the 10 best trading days had been missed, then the return would have almost halved to just £720. If the next 10 best trading days were also missed, then the return would have dropped to £475 (see Table 7.1).

Longer timescales confirm the message. Dr Kate Warne, whilst market strategist at Edward Jones in 2008, pointed out that if you had missed the 10 best trading days over the previous 39 years, the average annual return on your portfolio would fall to 5.6 per cent from 7.5 per cent. To put this into numbers, a £10,000 investment would have been worth £168,204 if it had remained invested between December 1968 and March 2008. But missing the best 10 trading days reduced the end value to £84,252 – an almost 50 per cent drop!

Table 7.1   Impact of timing the market

What happens if you miss the best days (10-year time frame)

30 Oct 2000- 29 Oct 2010	Whole time in market (£)	Less 10 best days (£)	Less 20 best days (£)	Less 30 best days (£)	Less 40 best days (£)
£1,000 invested into the FTSE All Share	1,330.01	719.70	475.13	336.27	249.08

Source: From Duncan, E. (2012), 'Act now', *What Investment*, May.

Now it could be said that an investor would have to be extremely unlucky for this to happen. But markets often make big moves when sentiment is poor and markets have fallen: in other words, when a lot of the bad news is in the price. And evidence from a number of unit trust managers suggest retail investors have a tendency to buy when the market has risen, and to sell when markets have fallen.

Often, investors sit on high cash piles for some time after markets have hit a low – they let past market movements influence investment behaviour. This is easy to criticise with the benefit of hindsight, but difficult to counter at the time. Yet it is precisely at these moments – with sentiment rock bottom – that markets tend to bounce. Investors are then often left behind. It is worth remembering that the single best trading day during the past 10–15 years occurred when the FTSE All Share rose 9.2 per cent on 24 November 2008, in the middle of the ballooning credit crisis and when investors' confidence was probably at its lowest level.

Another report by Blue Sky Asset Management in 2010[4] confirmed that investors rattled about market falls were failing to take advantage of cheaper prices. It argued that Fidelity's focus on the 10 best trading days was more relevant to day traders, rather than the average retail investor.

It therefore looked at the effect on returns if an investor had hoarded cash for one year after a market low, which it argued was the more typical behaviour of the private investor. And, having analysed bear markets in the UK since 1972, it found that such an approach would have reduced returns over the following four years by up to 75 per cent.

So missing some of the best trading days is not uncommon. The advice understandably given by advisers is that investors should reverse their normal behaviour and buy low and sell high. In doing so, investors should try to be more forward-looking and not be influenced by past events and the gloom that surrounds you. In other words, buy the future and not the past!

However, this is easier said than done. It is not easy for many investors to be buying when all hell is breaking loose. Instead, my advice is that investors should stay invested and ignore the small talk and chatter of the markets. Time in the market is more important than market timing. Market timing is a mug's game and, unless you are one of a very small number of investors who consistently get it right, best avoided.

In short, time is your friend. Ibbotson Associates analysed the S&P 500 since 1926 and concluded that an investor with a portfolio that mirrored the index would have lost money just 14 per cent of the time, based on five-year periods with dividends re-invested. The figure drops to 4 per cent over 10-year periods, whilst there would have been no losses at all over 15-year periods.

This is why investment is a long-term endeavour – the longer in the market, the better the chances of success. It is also why investors should stay invested and not try to second-guess volatility. Treat the market with respect and approach it with humility. If you stay loyal, it will reward you; but stray, and it will punish you. Repeat again: market timing is less important than time in the market!

However, there is one downside with this rule: the longer in the market, the greater the chance of experiencing a market crash. And crashes are painful when they happen. The stock market fell by a quarter in 1973, and then by a further half in 1974. On Black Monday in October 1987, the FTSE 100 fell 22 per cent in one day. In 2008, the FTSE 100 lost around a third of its value. These setbacks can be particularly galling if you were about to liquidate a portfolio because objectives had been met. The risk of this happening can never be eliminated, but a couple of strategies pursued together can help reduce the chances of a market collapse completely scuppering plans:

1 You should gradually start liquidating a portfolio some time before the money is required or objectives have been met (see 'Reaching goals' at the end of this chapter).

2 As an investor, you should always diversify your portfolio.

Diversification

The aim of diversification is to reduce portfolio risk by investing in 'uncorrelated' asset classes. These are assets that tend not to move in the same direction over the same period. The theory is that you should not put all your eggs in one basket, and that by apportioning a portfolio between non-correlated assets one is reducing risk – but not eliminating it – should markets fall.

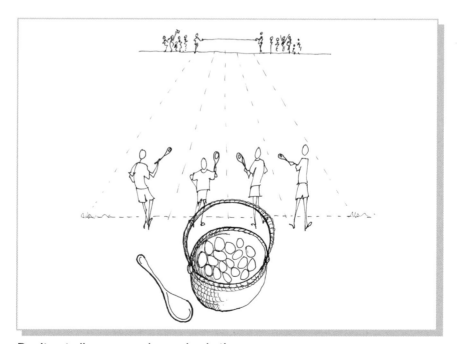

Don't put all your eggs in one basket!

If two shares move together – for example, pharmaceutical stocks such as GlaxoSmithKline and AstraZeneca – it is said they are highly correlated. However, holding a 'defensive' stock such as Glaxo (demand for medical treatment tends to be immune to economic swings) and a more 'cyclical' stock such as Barclays (demand for banking services are more geared to the economy) should reduce risk because they are less likely to fall together.

But how many individual equities should be held to diversify properly? James Montier suggested a few years ago that 32 stocks would eliminate 96 per cent of non-market risk (all but a stock-market crash). Research confirms that 30–40 holdings achieve the most diversification benefits.

Yet the average US fund manager holds anything between 100–160 stocks, which many consider excessive. The reason is that many want to replicate, as far as possible, the market and therefore market returns, in order not to underperform their peers. As the legendary investor Sir John Templeton once noted, the poor performance of US mutual (retail) funds was primarily due to 'institutional factors that encourage them to over diversify' and so incur high dealing costs.

So much for local equity markets. It is generally recognised that, within the equity asset class, you should diversify overseas. In a research paper, 'International Diversification Works (Eventually)', C. Asness, R. Israelov and J. Liew from AQR Capital Management compared the performance of local portfolios from 22 countries with globally diversified ones, covering the period 1950–2008.[5] The conclusion was that, for periods longer than five years, global funds performed significantly better during global crashes.

This reflects the fact that, whilst crashes drag down all markets in the short term, economic performance varies across countries over the longer term. International exposure therefore reduces risk as the fortunes of the portfolio are not riding on just one economy. As if to emphasise the point, portfolios in the US lost money over the first decade of this century, whilst emerging market equities generated returns of around 10 per cent a year.

However, equities – whether local or global – are only one asset class. There are others. Most typically these are bonds, real assets (such as gold, rare stamps or fine wine), genuine wealth-preserving absolute-return funds, property, commodities, private equity and cash. The price of such assets is influenced by different economic factors at different times.

For example, if there was an economic slump and deflationary fear, then typically bonds and cash would perform relatively well. If, on the other hand, economic growth surprised on the upside and inflation looked set to rise modestly, then equities and real assets would typically outperform.

During turbulent markets, it would be very unlikely for all these asset classes to fall in the same direction. Even during the equity sell-off in 2008, at the height of the credit crunch, perceived safe havens such as government bonds and good-quality corporate debt performed well. Meanwhile, cash produced a positive return. But some so-called 'equity diversifiers' did not live up to their billing. Many hedge funds, so called because they are meant to protect wealth in all markets, sank faster than other equity-based investments. Only a small minority honoured their title.

The answer is to keep it simple. Do not over diversify. As the US investor Warren Buffett once said, 'Wide diversification is only used when investors do not understand what they are doing.' The main diversification is between equities and bonds – asset classes driven by very different economic forces. And be wary of exotic 'alternative' assets classes such as hedge funds that promise the earth. If it sounds too good to be true, then it probably is.

To emphasise the point, a few years ago *MoneyWeek* discussed an *FT* article that highlighted a report by James Norton of Evolve Financial Planning.[6] It suggested that assets split 60/40 between the FTSE All-Share and the Citi Bond index between 1988 and 2008 would have earned 8.8 per cent a year. If the portfolio was widened to eight asset classes then the figure rises to 9.9 per cent for very little extra risk. Go beyond that and you add little extra return for a lot more risk.

Furthermore, costs go up the more asset classes are held, especially if you invest in the more exotic classes such as hedge funds, rare wine and stamps, or private equity. The best approach is to diversify across three or four asset classes at most. Investors are better off getting a good level of exposure to a small group of assets that represent attractive value than trying to spread the portfolio too thinly.

Of course, most asset classes are represented by investment trusts – the exception being certain 'real' assets such as gold and silver, and to a lesser extent government bonds. These can be accessed through exchange-traded funds (ETFs). So there is no reason why trust portfolios cannot be adequately diversified. The two *Investors Chronicle* trust portfolios I manage only have four asset classes: equities and bonds (mostly corporate) are the main ones, with commercial property, cash and perhaps commodities/gold (via mining shares) bringing up the rear.

Reinvesting dividends

I have highlighted why it is better to stay invested over the longer term, and not to trade market volatility in the hope of making short-term capital gains. But there is another reason not to stay out of the markets for extended periods. Over the longer term, it is dividends – and not capital gains – that produce the vast majority of market returns. Finding and re-investing dividends is the key to healthy returns.

The very useful annual Equity Gilt Study from Barclays Capital illustrates the point.

Example

£100 invested in UK stocks at the end of 1899 would have been worth £180 in real terms (after inflation) at the end of 2010, if dividends had not been reinvested. But with dividends reinvested, the figure shoots up to £24,133 – a very real increase. Shorter time frames since 1945 also confirm the story. (See Table 7.2.)

Table 7.2	2011 value of £100 invested in 1899 and 1945, comparing dividends reinvested and not reinvested	
Income reinvested	1899	£24,133
	1945	£4,370
Without reinvested income	1899	£180
	1945	£255

This validity of this message is not confined to UK markets. The US Dow Jones index was worth the same in 1992 as at the peak in 1929 in real terms, if dividends were not included – and the same in March 2009 as in 1966.

Legendary investor Jeremy Siegel put it another way in his book *The Future for Investors* (Crown Business, 2005). He calculated that, over a 130-year period, as much as 97 per cent of the total return from US stocks came from reinvested dividends. The figures were eye-opening. $1,000 invested in 1871 would have been worth $243,386 by 2003. Had dividends been reinvested, the figure rose to $7,947,930!

The message is clear: if you want to succeed over the longer term then do not spend your dividends. Almost every research paper proves that reinvesting dividends is the best way to grow wealth over time – and is less risky than trying to make short-term trades in the hope of crystallising capital gains. To access these dividends, you must stay invested.

And the good news at the moment is that companies are in good financial health. Whereas governments and consumers are mired in debt that will take years to work off, corporate balance sheets are healthy. A study by Capita Registrars[7] has shown that dividends paid to shareholders by UK-listed companies surged to an all-time high of £41.4 billion in the first half of 2012. This was 21 per cent higher than 2011 and well above the previous high of £34.5 billion in the first half of 2008.

Analysis suggests healthy dividend growth is not just a recent phenomenon. The 2012 Barclays Equity Gilt Study highlights that, while there have been fluctuations, dividends have tended to increase over the longer term. Meanwhile, looking forward, corporate balance sheets are set to strengthen steadily over the next few years. This should enhance their ability to pay increased dividends.

Regular rebalancing

Investors should never be complacent about the market. No matter how well a portfolio is performing, you should always treat it with respect for it can often surprise. And almost regardless of economic or market outlook, history suggests investors should regularly rebalance their portfolios.

Rebalancing is one of the first principles of investing, and yet it is often over-looked. The concept is simple. If a 60/40 bond/equity split is adopted and equities then have a very good run relative to bonds, you could end the period with a 70/30 split. This is because the value of the equities has increased more than your bonds. Evidence suggests that it pays to rebalance this portfolio – back to the 60/40 split – provided your risk profile and investment objectives remain unchanged.

Rebalancing worked well during the recent downturn. In the period 2007–09, a portfolio starting with a 60/40 split would have lost 37 per cent if unbalanced, compared to a loss of 30 per cent if balanced annually. However, this time frame is too short to prove the principle worthwhile.

Longer-term case histories are more revealing. Forbes has shown that £10,000 invested by way of a 60/40 split in the US in 1985, and rebalanced annually, would have been worth $97,000 in 2010. By comparison, an unbalanced portfolio would have been worth $89,000.

What is also noteworthy is that the rebalanced portfolio particularly protected investors better when markets fell significantly – which is logical. Over the longer term, shares have performed better than bonds. Therefore, rebalancing will typically involve selling equities and buying bonds. When markets fall, usually shares suffer most as good-quality bonds are seen as a safe haven. Rebalancing therefore reduces the impact. Investors with higher-risk portfolios take note. Unbalanced portfolios can seriously increase the risk profile of unguarded investors – who only realise their error too late when markets fall.

Rebalancing is recommended but be careful not to do it too often, because dealing costs eat into performance. City fund managers tend to rebalance on a quarterly basis, but their dealing costs are far lower. An annual rebalance is probably about right for most private investors, depending of course on how markets have performed. Such a rebalancing exercise is also a good time to revisit investment strategy, and to check it is still on course to meet objectives.

Reaching investment goals

During the life cycle of a portfolio, much care and attention is given to establishing and monitoring the component parts in the hope of healthy returns. This is perfectly right and understandable. However, as you approach the attainment of investment goals or a time when money is required, then as much care should be taken in the planning of this liquidation as it is in the running of the portfolio. It is an obvious point to make, but one that is nevertheless sometimes forgotten both by investors and managers alike.

Investors must always have in the back of their minds the consequences to them of a market crash. These are rare but largely unpredictable. This is particularly the case as you approach the finishing line. It is a great shame when, after many years of productive investing, a market setback severely dents overall gains just as investment goals are being reached. There are two answers to this, usually working in tandem.

Earlier in the chapter we discussed the merits of diversification. The second answer is to spread the liquidation over time as the finishing line approaches. This can be done over a matter of months, or even years if the portfolio has been running for a long time.

As to the precise method, you can obviously stagger sales in equal measure across all holdings so the portfolio largely retains its balance and shape as it is drawn down, or one can time sales of different holdings and assets according to perceived value and the economic backdrop. But whichever method or methods is chosen, it is important to execute this staged liquidation and then allow the balance of the holdings to carry the portfolio over the line, even though this may take a little longer in reaching.

Peace of mind should not be under estimated, particularly if this comes at the end of a long investment journey!

8

Other investment secrets

Having covered the basics when it comes to successful investing, this chapter will highlight some other pointers that you may find helpful when constructing and/or monitoring a portfolio, whether run by your manager or yourself. I start with what I consider to be the most important.

Sentiment versus fundamentals

If I had to sum up in one sentence the secret of successful investing, I would suggest 'to know when sentiment and fundamentals part company, and then to have the courage to act'. When market sentiment runs too far ahead relative to the asset's fundamentals – in other words, investors are pushing the price up beyond its worth – then the time has come to sell. Conversely, when sentiment trails fundamentals – the market is ignoring and so undervaluing the asset's prospects – then that is the time to buy.

It sounds easy, but it is not. First, you must identify when the market has got it wrong – when the price is not reflecting reality. You must believe that you have identified a mispricing which the collective wisdom of the market has missed. And then, the investor must ignore the perceived wisdom of fellow investors and deal in the market – to put to the test the courage of your own convictions. Sometimes it can take nerves of steel, particularly when buying on a market fall.

A successful investor must be prepared to be a contrarian – to think differently. It requires a resolute character who can withstand peer pressure and remain true to a conviction even if short-term results are disappointing. Such investors must stand back from the noise and clatter of the markets, and marry up their investment objectives with a calm assessment of what they believe assets are worth. Whichever benchmarks you apply, it can only be beaten by deviating from it. As Sir John Templeton once said, 'It is impossible to produce superior performance unless you do something different from the majority.'

Many commentators have suggested markets are driven by greed and fear. Greed pushes prices up to levels beyond the underlying assets' worth, in the hope that profits can be maximised – taking comfort from the fact the market itself is doing likewise en route. There is always comfort in numbers. Meanwhile, fear pushes prices down to levels below the assets' worth, assisted by the fact investors dislike losing money more than they like making it. Such concern is again perhaps influenced by the actions of those around you – a free-falling market must know something.

Generally speaking, contrarian investors tend to be value investors, because unloved assets are sought whilst the market's darlings are sold. Obtaining value provides a margin of comfort: buying at a decent discount to an asset's estimated worth offers protection against being wrong. And the benefit of contrarian investing has been illustrated through various studies showing that the stocks professional fund managers are selling usually outperform the ones they are buying.

Some have suggested it can be difficult for 'small' investors to compete with big players such as the pension funds and banks. After all, they have many advantages including the latest technology. I would disagree. The playing field is fairly level. The small investor has both advantages and disadvantages relative to professional fund managers.

Small investor disadvantages

The disadvantages for small investors include poor access to market information and to those running the underlying investments, whether they are company directors or the managers who run the underlying open- or closed-ended funds. But this is less a disadvantage than it might first appear. There are no shortage of good publications and websites that undertake detailed interviews and analysis of such assets. Furthermore, the companies and funds themselves are doing more to reach out to shareholders – existing and potential – for it is in their interests to do so. And if this were the determining factor in deciding whether managers outperformed their markets then most would, but it is not – because most do not.

Small investor advantages

Meanwhile, small investors have many advantages that should not be underestimated. First, and most importantly, they have time. Many professional fund managers have short-term horizons – quarterly meetings with trustees or actuaries focus the mind on three-monthly returns. There is therefore a constant pressure to shadow benchmarks and markets generally – to over-diversify or to replicate – for fear of being out on a limb and wrong.

Small investors are free of this restraint. They can afford to take a longer term view, and therefore stand a better chance of recognising mispricing and capitalising from it. Patience is often rewarded, perhaps because unloved assets can often be deeply discounted by the market. This is why patience is an asset. If, on the other hand, you are naturally impatient then perhaps you should seek your returns elsewhere. As the legendary investor Ben Graham once wrote: 'Undervaluations caused by neglect or prejudice may persist for an inconveniently long time and the same applies to inflated prices caused by over-enthusiasm or artificial stimulants.'[1]

Being free of this restraint also helps in other ways. Earlier sections covered the importance of staying invested until investment objectives had been attained. Greed and fear are natural human instincts, and they encourage fund managers to take short-term positions which, with the benefit of hindsight, are wrong. All the evidence suggests it is best to stick with the market over the longer term. Naturally, you can tweak things a bit. But, by and large, stay loyal to the market and it will reward you. Staying loyal also means investors reap the full reward of market dividends, which have a disproportionate benefit to overall returns. These advantages far outweigh the disadvantages.

Using the discount

Investment trusts are ideally suited to help the 'small' investor in this respect. Positive or negative sentiment towards an underlying trust and/or the market in general very often shows itself through the extent of the discount. The market will always present opportunities and risks that are often exaggerated by the fluctuation of discounts. Therein lies the investor's opportunity. And like good contrarian investors, those investing in investment trusts are natural value investors for they are looking for good quality trusts on a wider-than-normal discount – aiming to buy assets below their worth because of market sentiment.

The ideal purchase is when a trust, with a manager who has a good long-term track record and who is still in place, stands at a wider than average discount, possibly because the sector or manager is out of favour short term or the market is wobbly. It is worth remembering that many investors place too much emphasis on 'flavour of the month' investment themes and short-term performance when buying funds, often investing just as performance peaks. Better to focus on the longer-term track record of a good manager and ignore the short term negative sentiment and noise. The ideal sale is when a trust's discount has narrowed substantially from its average, perhaps because the market has got over-excited about prospects, yet factors such as a change of manager suggest caution.

Always remember though that these transactions should be based on long-term horizons. They should typically influence the timing as to when to introduce a long-term holding or to sell if close to realising overall investment objectives, and should not represent short-term trading positions. As earlier chapters have made clear, choosing a trust with good long-term performance is generally a far better contributor to overall returns than constant dealing in an attempt to take advantage of short-term swings in discounts or the twists and turns of the market.

Keep it simple and cheap

Financial professionals have a habit of unduly complicating products and services. If there is one message in this book, it is that investment is best kept simple to succeed. Complexity adds cost, risks confusion and usually hinders performance. This plays out at two levels. The previous chapter highlighted the importance of not diversifying your portfolios too much via different asset classes – in many respects, the smaller the number, the better.

But investors should also avoid investing in overly complicated products, particularly if they are difficult to understand. Therefore, avoid hedge funds and absolute return funds, structured products, multi-manager funds and any other investment vehicle that has high costs and poor transparency. History has shown they tend not to live up to expectations.

The high costs of such products are a particular negative. Allied to keeping it simple, investors should always try to keep it cheap, whether you are considering individual funds, diversification or the possibility of a raft of complicated products to complement portfolios in the hope of higher returns or certainty.

This message deserves repeating. Picking complicated products can easily load a further 1.5 per cent of costs onto portfolios. This does not sound much, but it can have a devastating effect on performance.

Example

Assume you take a 40-year horizon, and invest £100 a month in a few investment trusts, perhaps broadening the range as the portfolio gets bigger but always sticking with this monthly sum. Also assume the portfolio produces a 5 per cent return a year, which is not unreasonable given past returns. After 40 years, the trust portfolio will be worth £150,000. However, if you had added a further layer of costs of 1.5 per cent a year, the portfolio's worth would have sunk to just £105,000.

In short, keep your investing simple. Ignore the clever marketing of products that come with high costs and little transparency. Stick with straightforward investment trusts and exchange-traded funds (ETFs). If you are unsure whether to be in the market at all, then play safe and stick your money in a bank or cash ISA.

Multi-manager funds

By way of illustration, let us look at multi-manager funds, or funds of funds as they are also known. These are products where a manager will manage a portfolio of funds – usually open-ended and with at least some home-grown – and charge investors an additional fee for doing so. Such multi-manager funds have been popular, and it is easy to understand why. They were seen as a one-stop shop by financial advisers by providing a simple way of outsourcing portfolio management to respected fund management companies. They also deferred capital gains tax (CGT) because the multi-managers made changes to portfolios within their wrappers which did not attract CGT.

However, research published by *Money Management* shows that investors have lost out through poor performance and high fees – despite the promise of diversified growth and lower risk.

Performance figures published at the end of 2011 show that the average annual growth rate for multi-manager funds in the IMA Active Managed sector over five years was just 1.6 per cent compared with an average of 2.3 per cent for all funds (see Table 8.1). The picture looks slightly better over 10 years with figures of 5.3 per cent and 5.2 per cent respectively. However, when looking at the IMA UK All Companies sector, these multi-manager funds returned just 0.1 per cent after five years compared to a sector average of 1.4 per cent. Here the picture does not improve over 10 years – these funds continue to lag behind the sector average with returns of 3.9 per cent and 4.5 per cent respectively.

The problem with these products is the high cost through double-charging – investors pay both fees charged by the underlying managers of the funds held in the portfolios and those charged by the multi-manager picking the funds. It makes for a heady cocktail of costs. The total expense ratio (TER) for many multi-managers can be 1.5–2 per cent or more, which is an additional charge on top of the underlying portfolio fund's charge of around 1.5 per cent. This layering of charges means the bar has been raised significantly before investors can enjoy the benefit of good performance, as the statistics would seem to confirm.

Because of these high charges and consequential mediocre performance, I would expect multi-manager funds to struggle as the Retail Distribution Review (RDR) encourages managers and investors alike to pay closer attention to fees.

Table 8.1 Multi-manager funds: best and worst in IMA Active Managed sector, to September 2011

	Total expense ratio (%)	Value of £1,000 over (£)				Annual growth rate (%)	
		one year	three years	five years	10 years	Five years	10 years
Top five performers							
Margetts Venture Strategy	1.62	982	1,322	1,414	2,445	7.2	9.4
Pru Growth Trust	1.65	1,000	1,293	1,399	2,238	6.9	8.4
M&G Managed Growth	1.67	1,033	1,246	1,395	2,246	6.9	8.4
Jupiter Merlin Growth Portfolio	2.57	1,031	1,283	1,313	2,275	5.6	8.6
Threadneedle Nav Growth	1.53	1,014	1,251	1,251	1,690	4.6	5.4
Bottom five performers							
Barclays Adventurous Growth	2.33	966	1,035	876	1,091	-2.6	0.9
Insight Inv Divers Dynamic	2.35	967	875	903	1,279	-2.0	2.5
CF Danske Active Growth	2.59	956	1,062	964	-	-0.7	-
Henderson Global Strategic Capital	1.50	1,048	1,148	966	1,693	-0.7	5.4
TB Wise Income	2.15	1,010	1,148	973	-	-0.5	-
Average (multi-manager funds in sector)		1,000	1,150	1,090	1,700	1.6	5.3
Average (all funds in sector)		1,006	1,149	1,124	1,685	2.3	5.2

Source: From Clarke, G. (2011), 'Multi-manager funds serve up few benefits', The Financial Times, 19–20 November © The Financial Times Limited. All rights reserved.

Hedge funds

The situation regarding hedge funds, and their investment cousins the absolute-return funds (ARFs), is little different. Their purpose is to provide capital protection and deliver steady, if unexciting, returns with low correlation to underlying markets. They promise growth whatever the market conditions, and yet most failed to achieve this when the markets fell in 2008. There were exceptions of course – funds managed by Brevan Howard and BlueCrest were notable exceptions in generating impressive capital growth. But the majority failed.

Meanwhile, performance when markets are rising still leave investors with questions. 2012 is a case in point. Some estimates suggest that the average hedge fund produced a 3 per cent gain. This compares with a 13 per cent gain in the world equity market.

Assessing the longer-term performance of this group of products is not easy. The widely used HFRX Global Hedge Fund index, which weights each strategy by assets, gives an average annual total return (net of fees) of 7.3 per cent between 1998 and 2010. By comparison, the S&P 500 and US Treasuries produced total returns of 5.9 per cent and 3.0 per cent respectively. So far so good – investors might think such performance was worth paying the high fees for.

But these figures tend to ignore the fact that the better performance years were the early ones when the industry was small. Performance deteriorated as the industry grew. And most investors came to hedge funds in the later years when these funds were performing less well – a fact not helped by the extent of losses in 2008 when the industry might have lost more money than all the profits it had generated in the previous 10 years.

This is illustrated by Figure 8.1, featured in Simon Lack's recent book *The Hedge Fund Mirage* (2012), which shows the annual percentage return of the industry between 1998 and 2010.

Lack believes performance is better assessed by using the internal rate of return (IRR), which gives greater prominence to performance weighted by assets rather than simply looking at annualised returns. This performance measure is widely used by private equity and property investors. Over the 1998–2010 period, IRR figures from the alternative-investment database BarclayHedge suggest a more sombre figure of 2.1 per cent.

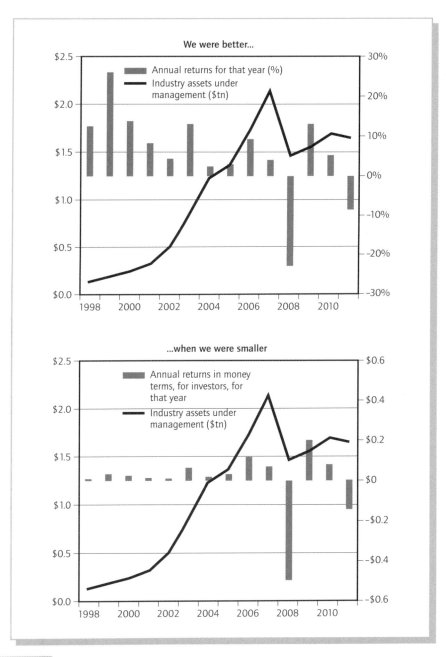

Figure 8.1   **Hedge fund industry performance**

Source: Securities and Investment Review, August 2012.

Meanwhile, performance once again is not helped by very high fees. Some hedge funds charge '2 and 20', meaning a 2 per cent fee of funds under management plus a 20 per cent performance fee. Some funds of hedge funds then charge a '1 and 10' on top. It is therefore perhaps no surprise that Lack's analysis shows that, between 1998 and 2010, hedge fund managers kept 84 per cent of the profits they made.

This then begs the question as to why these funds have been so popular. Why is it that investors have flocked to their standard, despite the under-performance and high fees? After all, these are not novice investors: around two-thirds of hedge funds' assets belong to charitable, pension and other institutional funds. These are investors who know their stuff. I recently heard an interesting personal story that may cast some light on this question.

> *A fund manager once pitched for new business to a lawyer who represented a large family trust. The trust wanted a new investment approach. The presentation outlined a simple, balanced and low-cost portfolio. Other managers also pitched, but their investment strategies were more complicated and costly. The lawyer then told the manager in question that the trust had rejected his portfolio strategy – one key reason being it was too simple. The manager then re-engineered his proposal by tweaking the return, risk and cost numbers up a little. He also suggested the new strategy was overseen by very clever people who would not reveal their methods. The manager won the trust.*

It is harsh to suggest that hedge funds play on human frailty, but there is a tendency in our natures to want to believe success can only be secured by complicated methods – otherwise, why would everyone not be succeeding. This may be true in other fields of human endeavour, but not when it comes to investment. Investors need to remember, they stand a better chance of securing portfolio success if strategies are kept simple and therefore cheap.

This is not to deny some investors have been well served by the industry – particularly those who were early to participate. But the majority of investors would do well to look closely at performance since the asset class has become an established part of the investment universe. I cannot help but feel that those who have used hedge funds in recent years have not been well served and consequently, until fees become more reasonable and they deliver promised performance, the industry should be avoided.

Structured products

Structured products promise to protect investors' capital against market volatility and pay out a pre-determined sum depending on how well the underlying asset class or index – typically the FTSE 100 – has performed. The payout is usually based on two possible outcomes – a rise or fall in the nominated index – and they have a fixed investment term. FTSE 100-linked structured products in particular usually pay out either a fixed return when the market falls, or your capital plus a percentage (e.g. 60 per cent) of the capital gain achieved by the index, usually minus fees. They are marketed as a way of protecting against market volatility, whilst providing a degree of assurance about investment returns. As such, they have proved popular.

I would advise caution. As with all these sorts of products, they are complex and investors need to understand the risks, so study the small print. It is important to understand the margins of safety when it comes to the extent of your losses and gains when markets move. With many of these products, if the market falls less than 40–50 per cent then the initial sum invested is recouped, but if the market fall exceeds this figure then often your initial capital suffers by the same proportion. Conversely, be aware that in many cases the 'bonus' element will not be available if the FTSE 100 index is but just one point off its opening level.

Meanwhile, such products are inflexible. Heavy penalty clauses usually exist if investors cash in early. The current investment climate is fluid to say the least, with very possibly higher inflation due. Locking up capital for up to five years is not wise in such a scenario. Meanwhile, whatever 'bonus' is paid by these products is less attractive when you consider that no dividends or interest is paid over the life of the product. An investment trust that performs well can yield more than 4 per cent and therefore, aided by compound interest, will produce income equivalent to almost half the 'bonus' over five years.

In addition, they are expensive. The more complicated the product, the pricier it will be. Fees of 3 per cent are not uncommon and they are usually taken up front. This compares to a FTSE 100 ETF charging less than 0.5 per cent and a good-performing investment trust between 1 per cent and 1.5 per cent a year.

Finally, you should always consider the default risk. Most of these products are backed or sponsored by a third party, usually a bank. And most banks are perfectly sound with good credit ratings. However, it is worth remembering that a range of structured products were affected by the collapse of their sponsor Lehman Brothers in 2008 – a bank which also had a good credit rating.

Worse still, there is a risk that some products will not be covered by the Financial Services Compensation Scheme. Santander, the Spanish bank, last year had to write apologising to all its customers who had invested £2.7 billion into 178,000 complicated structured products between October 2008 and January 2010. The reason was that the bank's Guaranteed Capital Plus and Guaranteed Growth Plans – offering various payouts depending on FTSE 100 returns over 3.75 and 5.5 years – were not covered, and it had failed to point this out at the time.

Structured products are an expensive why to hedge an investor's own indecision. Essentially two types of people are attracted to these products: those who really should not take on any risk, and those who could afford to do so. If you are in the first camp or are bearish, then place your cash in a bank account or cash ISA. If you are in the second, buy an investment trust or two. But do not be left paying for the expensive luxury of indecision – others are sure to profit.

Ignore forecasts

The renowned economist J.K. Galbraith once said: 'Pundits forecast not because they know, but because they are asked.' History suggests these forecasts are rarely right. As such, successful investors have a healthy and sceptical disregard for forecasts – whether they be company, market or economic. This tallies with their contrarian streak, in that one prerequisite to behaving differently is to ignore the noise and clatter of consensus forecasts as to the outlook.

At a company or fund level, the successful investors are asking what could go wrong – what is the downside with holding this stock? They need to understand the potential risks. This sceptical approach often uncovers all sorts of negatives not appreciated. It certainly reduces the risk of unpleasant surprises, and encourages a better appreciation of the risk–reward balance. Company forecasts are ignored. The default position for these investors is not to own the stock.

This approach compares with those professional fund managers who are more focused on relative performance – they are concerned with tracking, and not being left behind by their peers. This encourages a different approach: why should I not own this stock? Non-ownership is less of a possibility – sceptism takes a back seat.

Successful investors also tend to ignore the broader economic forecasts. It is questionable why so much effort is expended towards an activity which has so little value and little chance of success. Simply calculating the probabilities is revealing.

Even if you have a two-thirds chance of getting right each forecast relating to (1) economic growth, (2) the path of interest rates, and (3) which sectors will benefit from the predicted environment, then this still only means you have a 30 per cent chance of getting all three right. And these odds do not even take into account the need to make a correct stock/trust decision. The message is to ignore forecasts and rely on your own research and intuition.

As for market forecasts, the successful investor is wary – and right to be so. End-of-year forecasts are rarely consistently right. The many forecasters who use the complex maths of Black and Scholes or some other such calculations would do better studying history. The successful investor fully appreciates Sir John Templeton's observation that 'This time is different' are the four most dangerous words in investing – whatever rocket-science black box has produced the verdict.

The magic of compound interest

Last but not least, it is wise to start investing as early as you can afford. This is because, as Einstein allegedly said, compound interest is the eighth wonder of the world.

Compounding is the regular reinvesting of interest or dividends to the original sum invested with the effect of creating higher total returns (capital gains and income) over time. The fact that interest/dividends is reinvested and future interest is paid both on the original sum and the accumulated interest makes for a significant improvement in total returns over the longer term – compared to if interest on the original sum only was reinvested (known as straight or simple interest).

But for compound interest to work its magic, two ingredients are required – lots of time and a good rate of return. If you invest £100 a month for 10 years earnings 3 per cent a year, which is added back to the pot, then the total pot will be worth £14,009. Leave the process to run for 20 years and the total pot is worth £32,912. Patience brings its own rewards.

But if the rate of return was to rise from 3 per cent to 7.5 per cent (the average long-term return for US equities) over the periods in question, then this has a dramatic effect on the final figures. The £100 a month invested over 20 years creates a total pot worth £135,587. Leave it for 40 years and the pot is worth £304,272. The challenge is to achieve this higher rate of return.

But the lesson is simple. The earlier you start investing, the greater the compounding effect in your favour, and the bigger the final pot will become. By its very nature, the best of the magic is achieved towards the end of a decent period of time. Start early, be patient and try not to interrupt the magic of compounding.

The *Investors Chronicle* portfolios

Theories and words are fine, but the true test comes when putting these into action. This is the reason for the two *Investors Chronicle* portfolios, and my monthly column explaining how they are managed and why any changes are made.

The rationale

The columns were born out of a frustration that, while there was no shortage of good financial commentary about markets in general and equities in isolation, there was and remains precious little to help investors monitor or manage their portfolios as a whole. Good investment is not simply about getting a series of separate trades more right than wrong – difficult though some find that. It is about weaving these together in a coherent strategy via a portfolio that correctly balances risk with reward, geography with theme, capital growth with income, etc., so that objectives are reached.

These Growth and Income portfolios have been running since the beginning of 2009. They are designed to help investors – both novice and expert – to either run their own portfolios or monitor those who manage their portfolios. Almost uniquely, these portfolios actually exist (they are not virtual) and are benchmarked so investors can see how well they are performing against objective measures.

Each month the column highlights any changes to the portfolios – although some months there are none. In a very transparent manner, both successes and failures are shared with the reader – as ever, the aim being to get more decisions right than wrong! In explaining the logic behind the changes, the column focuses on key investment themes and strategies, always trying to sift the short-term noise and clatter of the markets from what is important on a longer-term view.

The column singles out investment trusts that are looking attractive and are best placed to harness these themes, whilst monitoring the progress of existing holdings. The trust managers at the coal face are doing the hard work. I aim to add value through choice of trusts, asset allocation and themes. In the one or two areas where assets are not strongly represented by trusts – bonds are one example – I use exchange-traded funds (ETFs). So far, both portfolios have performed well relative to their benchmarks, but as I hope you have realised by now, investors should never be complacent.

I approach the column in the same manner as if I were updating a client as to progress. Except in this case, the update is monthly instead of quarterly or half-yearly. As such there is no reason why investors could not run their portfolios by simply adhering to this column's advice – providing of course the risk profiles, yields and benchmarks are broadly appropriate. An execution-only service, established by the reader, is the only prerequisite. If you fit into this bracket then this column saves you paying for an adviser or wealth manager!

The chosen benchmarks are the FTSE APCIMS private investor indices which are well recognised within the industry. These were set up by FTSE International and the Association of Private Client Investment Managers and Stockbrokers (APCIMS) to help private investors benchmark their investment performance. There are three indices: Growth, Income and Balanced. I chose the Growth and Income benchmarks for the two portfolios as the Balanced falls between the two, and my experience suggests most investors want to achieve one of these two objectives.

Chapter 6 contains pie charts of the two illustrating their components (see Figure 6.1), but this is shown here in tabular form (see Table 9.1).

Table 9.1   Latest percentage components of the two indices

	FTSE APCIMS Stock Market Income index %*	FTSE APCIMS Stock Market Growth index %*
UK equities – FTSE All-Share index	37.5	45.0
International equities – FTSE All-World ex UK index (£) **	17.5	37.5
Bonds – FTSE Gilts All-Stocks index	35.0	7.5
Cash – 7-day LIBOR*** -1%	5.0	2.5
Commercial property – FTSE All-UK Property index (NAV)	2.5	0.0
Hedge funds – FTSE APCIMS Hedge (Investment Trust) index	2.5	7.5
Total	**100.0**	**100.0**

*Effective 1 July 2013
**Replaced the FTSE World ex UK Index on 2 April 2012
***London Interbank Offered Rate

Another attraction with this series of benchmarks is that the various components are actual indices – the relevant markets – rather than estimates reflecting how well the industry in general has performed. As indicated previously, I remain suspicious of such peer group indices, believing that peer-like comparisons can encourage herd-like performance. The market indices themselves remain the best measure as to how an individual portfolio is performing. Monitoring how the herd performs is of marginal use in reaching one's investment goals.

A further attraction of these benchmarks is that, very occasionally, the asset allocations are changed in response to quarterly surveys to ensure they remain relevant to investors' needs.

Investment philosophy

Both portfolios adhere to the basics when it comes to successful investing. The starting point is that the investment approach aims to keep it simple and cheap. One of the key messages in *The FT Guide to Investment Trusts* is that investment does not have to be complex to be successful. Quite the opposite. Both portfolios tend to avoid multi-manager funds, hedge funds and structured products because of their high costs, complexity and typically disappointing performance. Such products may have a role in the very largest of portfolios, but I hope both *Investors Chronicle* portfolios have shown over the years that it pays to keep it simple and cheap.

Both portfolios tend to remain invested. As I have argued in previous chapters, trying to second-guess short-term market swings tends to be a mug's game. It can also be very costly if good days are missed. I therefore accept with grace the ups and downs. I accept the slightly higher volatility that comes with investment trusts – knowing that discounts will widen when the market struggles, and narrow when things go well. I do this knowing that trusts tend to outperform their open-ended cousins and the markets generally over the longer term.

This approach does not prevent me from occasionally 'tapping the tiller'. There have been periods when both portfolios have been overweight bonds or overweight equities relative to benchmarks. My last asset allocation change was during the Spring of 2012 when I felt sentiment was overly bearish and so, having been somewhat defensively positioned, both portfolios increased their exposure to equities. Having enjoyed the subsequent run in equity markets, I then rebalanced the portfolios. However, these asset allocation decisions have tended to be modest 'calls' as I dislike being out of the market – the market tends to reward those investors who remain loyal.

Both portfolios are usually rebalanced once a year, particularly following significant market moves. Rebalancing is one of the first principles of investment and yet many investors tend to overlook it. The example given above at the end of 2012 involved increasing the bond exposure in both portfolios by adding higher-yielding corporate bonds – funded from profits taken from equities.

The Growth portfolio has a slightly higher turnover rate as the universe of suitable stocks is much wider. The Income portfolio tends to be anchored in those trusts with a decent yield, and growth in income is an important factor. However, the aim is to keep portfolio turnover low because dealing charges eat into performance. The performance figures cited for both portfolios are net of all such charges.

Meanwhile, both portfolios are reasonably well diversified with varying exposure to three to four asset classes – bonds, equities, commercial property and cash. Within each asset class there are various shades of grey. For example, as globalisation gathers pace, most equities are highly correlated. Both portfolios have exposure to 'Frontier markets' (markets other than 'Developed' or 'Emerging') which have tended to display less correlation to the key markets, and indeed to themselves.

Furthermore, both portfolios reinvest their dividends – performance is measured on a total return basis, as are the benchmarks. We have seen previously the extent to which dividends account for the total return of equities over any meaningful timescale. Portfolio yields are updated each month with the performance figures.

Finally, I follow my own advice and tend not to allow market forecasts to guide my investment decisions. I keep an eye on economic analysis because understanding which parts of the world are growing faster than others is useful. Not because faster-growing economies necessarily lead to better performing markets – China's economy has grown at an average annual rate of 8–10 per cent during the past decade, yet its stockmarket has hardly advanced at all. But because faster-growing economies provide a richer, more profitable, pool of companies in which good fund managers can fish. The Far East is a good example – one where smaller company trusts in particular have performed well.

Whilst recognising that economic analysis is useful, I try to adhere to the most important investment principle of all – and that is to separate the fundamentals of an asset from the sentiment shown it by the market. This above all should guide you in your investment choices. If you are to outperform the market, then you have to do something different to the market.

An example is the UK smaller company sector where, for reasons explained in the next section, sentiment continues to trail fundamentals despite the sector outperforming the wider market – and this why you can still pick up excellent trusts on 15–20 per cent discounts.

But the point about sentiment versus fundamentals can operate at any level. For example, when sentiment was rock bottom during the eurozone crisis because it was being influenced by the poor economic outlook, the market was ignoring the many excellent companies on the continent that had large overseas earnings – particularly in the faster-growing emerging economies. Both stock markets and good fund managers were being unfairly penalised, and this presented a wonderful opportunity to pick up both cheaply – and the markets duly rewarded the brave.

However, it is true to say that such an approach can sometimes require patience, or a short-term catalyst to wake the market from its torpor!

Investment strategy

Both portfolios pursue common themes when it comes to asset allocation. My long-held mantra has been 'Go high, go deep, go east'. Both portfolios, relative to their respective benchmarks, reflect this strategy: they are overweight high-yielding equities and corporate bonds, overweight smaller companies, and overweight the Far East. Within bonds they are underweight gilts, and within equities they are underweight the UK and the US. This has influenced my strategy for some time – and it looks set to continue to do so in future.

Performance has been respectable (see Table 9.2) but one can never be complacent.

Table 9.2   Portfolio performance: 1 January 2009 to 1 June 2013

	Growth	Income
Portfolio total return [%]	105.7	87.9
APCIMS total return [%]	65.3	53.0
Relative performance [%]	40.4	34.9
Yield [%]	2.2	4.1

The APCIMS Growth and Income benchmarks are cited [Total Return]

The breakdown of holdings (rounded to the nearest half a per cent) at the time of writing is given in Table 9.3.

| Table 9.3 | Asset allocation and holdings listed |

Growth portfolio		Income portfolio	
Bonds		Bonds	
Ishares Corp Bond ex-Fin[£] ETF	7%	Ishares Corp Bond Fund[£] ETF	9.5%
New City High Yield IT	3%	Ishares Corp Bond ex-Fin[£] ETF	8.5%
UK Shares		New City High Yield IT	7%
Temple Bar IT	5.5%	City Merchants High Yield IT	6%
Finsbury Growth & Income IT	4.5%	Ishares Gilt[£] ETF	4%
Montanaro UK Smaller Cos IT	4%	Invesco Lev High Yield IT	3.5%
Henderson Smaller Cos IT	4%	UK Shares	
Schroder UK Mid Cap IT	3.5%	Temple Bar IT	6%
Perpetual Income and Growth IT	3%	Murray Income IT	5.5%
Throgmorton IT	2%	Henderson Smaller Cos IT	4%
International Shares		Schroder UK Mid Cap IT	3%
Ishares Japan Monthly £ hedged ETF	6%	Perpetual Income and Growth IT	3%
Baillie Gifford Japan IT	5.5%	International Shares	
European Assets IT	5.5%	European Assets IT	5%
Aberdeen Asian Income IT	4%	Murray International IT	4.5%
Schroder Oriental Income IT	3.5%	JPMorgan Japanese IT	4%
Jupiter European Opportunities IT	3.5%	Ishares DJ Emerging Mkts Div ETF	3.5%
Scottish Oriental Smaller Cos IT	3%	Scottish Oriental Smaller Cos IT	3%
Aberdeen Asian Smaller Cos IT	3%	BlackRock Frontiers IT	2%
BlackRock Frontiers IT	3%	Themes	
JPMorgan Emerging Mkts Income IT	2.5%	Worldwide Healthcare IT	6%
Themes		HICL Infrastructure IT	2.5%
Herald IT	5%	M&G High Income Inc Shares IT	2%
Worldwide Healthcare IT	5%	BlackRock Commodities Income IT	2%
The Biotech Growth IT	3.5%		

Growth portfolio		Income portfolio	
International Biotechnology IT	2.5%	Commercial Property	
Utilico Emerging Markets IT	1.5%	Standard Life Property Income IT	3%
City Natural Resources IT	1.5%	TR Property IT	2%
Commercial property		Cash	0.5%
Standard Life Property Income IT	2.5%	Total	100%
TR Property IT	2%		
Cash	0.5%		
Total	100%	[Holdings are rounded to the nearest 0.5%]	

Go high

The rationale for 'going high' is that interest rates are set to remain low for some time to come. The slowdown in the West is unusual: this is a deleveraging recession and not a destocking one which has more typically characterised recessions since Keynes' time. Traditionally, a good dose of Keynesian stimulus to encourage demand – using borrowed money if necessary – would have corrected the situation. This option is not available today. The hallmark of this recession is excessive debt – both governments and consumers have lived beyond their means. The cupboard is now bare, and it makes little economic sense to borrow your way out of debt.

The long-term solution is economic growth. But where are the much-needed supply-side reforms? Or the measures to encourage greater competitiveness and reduce taxation? Instead, the debt is simply being moved around the system, between governments and banks and back again.

In recognising their failure, governments have set upon the course of 'financial repression'. The objective is to create a little more inflation in order to help erode the debt over time – a policy pursued after the Second World War. This is being achieved by keeping interest rates artificially low at both ends of the yield curve.

This is easy at the short end because of the compliance of government-appointed central bankers. It is achievable at the longer end by forcing the big players, the pension funds and banks, to be buyers of government bonds through regulations such as asset/liability matching and capital adequacy ratios – and yields reflect this artificial demand. Savers are suffering as a result.

This is a dark art. Quantitative easing is also part of the script. But whether successful or not, interest rates will remain low for years – there is too much debt in the system and governments want to avoid default. In such an environment, good-yielding equities and corporate bonds will remain in demand – particularly those equities that can increase payouts. Meanwhile, overseas income will play a more prominent role in portfolios.

Go deep

As for the 'go deep' part of the strategy, I remain of the view that smaller companies globally will continue to do well relative to the wider markets – for reasons espoused in my *Investors Chronicle* column 'Still set on small caps' (3 September 2010). It used to be conventional thinking that investors should overweight smaller companies during an economic up-swing, but underweight the sector as the economy struggled. This thinking needs to be challenged.

Globalisation continues apace. As a result, portfolio diversification by means of geography will continue to decline in importance relative to global themes. The hunt is on for those themes that will reward investors. By and large, in such an environment, the UK smaller companies sector in particular has tended not to be on some investors' radar screens because of the perception that the sector is heavily reliant on the domestic economy, particularly manufacturing and building.

But this perception is slowing changing. The sector today has much more overseas exposure and is therefore less exposed to the twists and turns of the UK economy. Many smaller companies now generate more than half of their earnings overseas, and have exposure to a much wider selection of sectors at least in part because of the advances in technology. Those hunting global themes no longer automatically shun smaller companies. And at a time when economic growth in the UK and the West generally will be anaemic at best, the right global themes will produce superior returns for investors.

Another positive change for the sector is that, after the shock of BP and other large companies cutting their dividends, more investors are looking further down the market cap spectrum for income. And the potential is huge. Many smaller companies now have stronger balance sheets and yield as much as their larger brethren.

In short, better management and greater access to international markets, in part thanks to technology and globalisation, together with the sector generally remaining under researched, makes for a powerful combination for good fund managers.

There is another factor that should be considered. Investors tend not to like volatility – it leads to sleepless nights and is often associated with riskier investments – and independent financial advisers (IFAs) have long cited volatility as a reason to shun the investment trust sector as a whole. Yet sentiment towards the smaller companies sector may improve as the low-growth environment ushers in less-extreme economic swings and therefore lower sector volatility. Some 15–20 per cent discounts on many good-performing smaller company trusts provide a wonderful investment opportunity.

Go east

Finally, I am more convinced than ever that investors should 'go east' for superior returns. I buy into the emerging markets story in general. In the present low-growth environment, you will increasingly have to look overseas for both growth and income. And whilst accepting that the faster economic growth rates of the emerging markets will not always necessarily translate into better-performing stock markets, such growth does make it easier for good fund managers to find good companies.

Most investors have the vast majority of their assets in developed markets, with only a small percentage in emerging markets – typically around 5–10 per cent. This remains the consensus despite the attraction of these developing markets. This will change over time. Those investors who beat the consensus in realising this will be rewarded.

As Dr Mark Mobius, manager of Templeton Emerging Markets Investment Trust, put it a few years ago: 'The key is growth. Growth is higher [in emerging markets]. The most populated countries in the world are also the fastest growing.' Growth rates in China, India, Brazil and many other emerging markets will continue to beat the western world by some margin. And these larger countries are now being joined by a host a smaller 'frontier' markets such as Nigeria, Saudi Arabia and Vietnam.

Meanwhile, many of these markets are now less risky for investors. Governments in these developing countries are not burdened by high levels of debt, corporate governance has improved significantly and there is improving political stability. Such factors help stock-market valuations. Furthermore, policy makers in these emerging market countries are gradually realising they cannot rely on western consumption as much as they have done in the past. We are seeing a structural change. Those emerging markets driven by domestic demand and investment will do especially well.

And this is where the Far East comes in. Many emerging markets, but particularly in Asia, have young populations and high savings ratios – they have not been great spenders. This may be about to change. Low interest rates reducing the desire to save, combined with cash-rich governments investing in infrastructure and social welfare projects, will result in domestic spending increasing significantly. The region also benefits from a low entitlements culture and a work ethic. It is full of promise.

In the past, as we have seen, volatility has tended to put investors off. This volatility will remain despite the lower investment risks, but investors should embrace and exploit it. As I have suggested before, if volatility is a measure of risk then investors would always be underweight good opportunities. The debate is more about timing. Investors should view volatility as an opportunity and not a risk.

Balancing competing factors

In the search for good investment returns, there are usually competing factors that need to be accommodated – and these two portfolios are no different.

One is geography versus themes. As can be seen from the breakdown of holdings, both portfolios hold trusts under the benchmark headings of 'UK shares' and 'International shares'. This is widespread practice among wealth managers and advisers, because geography and currency are still important determinants of investment return. It still pays to specialise in a region as rich and diverse as Europe, for example, as it will host a very wide spectrum of companies, sectors and industries.

However, both portfolios also have holdings under the heading 'Themes' – this not being part of either benchmark. This is because, as globalisation continues to gather pace, the pursuit of themes will become a more important contributor to investment returns. An example is the biotech sector, where it is wise to adopt a global approach given the strength of the sector in the US, and to a lesser extent, Europe and Japan – despite their respective economies being under pressure.

And it is usually important to 'look through' the thematic trusts to ascertaining geographic exposure. For example, at the time of writing, both portfolios are underweight the US. But a cursory glance at the holdings would suggest no exposure at all – there being no direct 'geographical' holdings, unlike other regions of the world. Yet exposure to the US accounts for around 60 per cent of the Worldwide Healthcare Trust (WWH), which is a major thematic holding in both portfolios. Likewise, the holding of The Biotech Growth Trust (BIOG) in the Growth portfolio has an 85 per cent weighting in North America.

In balancing geography and themes, I tend to give greater weighting to geography. This is because those fund managers specialising in the world's countries and continents will already be pursuing some of these themes. It is advisable to at least get a feel as to how trust portfolios are slanted by accessing the monthly factsheets or report and accounts. Both portfolios therefore have greater total weightings under the 'UK' and 'International share' headings than they do pursuing themes.

Another competing factor is that between capital growth and income. Both portfolios recognise that dividends make up the lion's share of investment returns – as much as 97 per cent of the total return of the US market over the past 130 years, according to recent research. Both portfolios therefore have a healthy yield relative to their benchmarks, and this bias within the portfolios will continue while the 'Go high' element of the strategy remains in place.

The conventional thinking used to be that bonds – government or corporate – would provide the income, and equities the capital growth. This was particularly the case after 1959 when the yield on equities fell below that offered by government bonds for the first time since time immemorial. But as both portfolios testify, the choice does not necessarily have to be a straight one between capital or income. Sometimes you can have both. Both portfolios hold equity trusts which have decent yields and have performed well in capital terms. Some of the UK income and Far East income trusts have been stellar performers – the latter helped by a weakening pound.

Of course it is difficult to generate yield from certain themes such as technology and bioscience. But increasing numbers of companies around the world are paying out rising dividends – it is almost seen as the rite of passage toward greater credibility and access to the capital markets. And given sterling's tendency to depreciate against other currencies – something that will continue until the UK rediscovers its ability to manufacture goods for export – then this overseas income becomes of increasing value.

Furthermore, there are certain parts of the world where I expect to see excellent capital growth from the equity markets over the longer term – certainly exceeding mainstream markets – and yet which offer good dividends. The frontier markets are a good example. Yields here are healthy because valuations are cheap – something that will change over time.

Perhaps one final point should be made when balancing growth and income. Even when seeking a decent income is the first priority, an investor should not sacrifice completely the compelling growth stories. For example, the Income portfolio has exposure to UK and Far Eastern smaller companies, Japan, and healthcare and biotech despite their relatively low yields. My expectation is that, longer term, their total returns will reward investors. Short term, I am compensating in income for their inclusion by over-weighting bonds and other high-yielding assets.

A further competing factor when searching for good investment returns is that between risk and reward. How far does an investor embrace risk in search for higher returns? The answer is subject to much debate. It is widely accepted that you cannot access reward without risk. We have examined in previous chapters the extent to which equity markets in particular can be volatile – and how government bond markets have sometimes not been far behind. If volatility concerns you, then perhaps stock markets should be shunned.

The approach adopted by both portfolios is to accept volatility and invest for the long term. History is, after all, on our side. The equity markets tend to reward those who remain loyal and stay invested – and staying invested helps to access the ever-important dividends.

The Income portfolio is better insulated against volatility because it has a much higher weighting in lower-risk government and corporate bonds. The search for yield encourages this, particularly when it comes to corporate bonds. But both portfolios are also overweight higher-yielding equities both at home and abroad. Theoretically this should help reduce the risk and volatility when markets hit turbulent patches – decent yield can act as a cushion in uncertain times.

But the existence of discounts will result typically in volatility no matter the investment strategy. I hope both portfolios have illustrated over the years that, for the patient investor willing to take a long-term view, the rewards are worth waiting for!

A recent column

By way of illustration as to the nature of these columns, below is one I prepared earlier! It was published in February 2013 in the *Investors Chronicle*.

Japan: a once in a lifetime opportunity?

John Baron believes the Japanese equity market could be at a major turning point.

In last month's column, space did not allow me to explain why I had introduced Baillie Gifford Japan Trust (BGFD) into the Growth portfolio in December. Readers will know that both portfolios have tended to avoid Japan in the past, but the recent election of Shinzo Abe as Prime Minister could be a 'game-changer' – and not another false dawn.

False dawns

Japan's problems have been well known for years. The country is drowning in debt, and there are concerns as to its ability to pay the interest let alone the capital back. Around half of all government income is consumed by debt interest. A series of infrastructure initiatives over the years have failed to kick start the economy, and only added to the debt mountain.

And the debt keeps rising – government expenditure exceeds income. The deficit will be nearly 10% of GDP this year. The situation has not been helped by a sluggish economy. A stubbornly high exchange rate has hindered exports with trade surpluses now turning into deficits. Connected to all this, the economy is struggling with deflation.

Governments have needed to raise income but found it difficult. One reason is that the population is declining and getting older, and this costs money. In the past, the government has been helped with its borrowing by its citizens' tendency to buy bonds. But bond yields and savings rates are now very low. This road is nearing its end.

It is therefore little surprise the stockmarket has drifted for years. There has been no shortage of false dawns – with 20–40 per cent rallies being relatively common. But they have all petered out because of economic reality. Many believe the catalyst needed to break this cycle of economic malaise is inflation. Previous governments have shunned the idea – enter Shinzo Abe.

The 'Abe Trade'

On 16 December [2012], Japanese voters finally decided they had had enough of their deflationary predicament. The rapid deterioration in Japan's current account and its growing inability to finance her large budget deficits has this time forced political and policy change.

Shinzo Abe won a landslide election – a two-thirds majority – advocating an aggressive programme of fiscal stimulus, despite the size of the budget deficit, and almost unlimited monetary easing. Inflation is now the number one objective. He wants the Bank of Japan (BoJ) to instigate a 2 per cent inflation target, as compared to the present 1 per cent, and does not mind the extent of money printing it takes to get there. He has made it known that if the independent BoJ does not oblige, then he will rewrite the law so that he can fire the board.

An all-out attack on deflation is now being executed. Many have argued that the BoJ's deflation-fighting efforts in the past have been half-hearted. It has certainly lagged other central banks. Between mid-2008 and mid-2012 its balance sheet – reflecting assets bought with printed money – grew by only 7 per cent of GDP, compared to 14 per cent by the Bank of England and the ECB. There is scope for the BoJ to be more aggressive.

And the effect could be dramatic. Japan has been mired in deflation. Consumer prices are still at 1993 levels; this compares to a 60 per cent gain since then in the US. As a result, Japanese government bonds have been in a bull market for 20 years. Equities have disappointed. However, if rising inflation ends the bull market in bonds – and changes the mindset of the traditionally conservative Japanese investors – the money currently flowing into bonds will need a new home. Where else but equities? After all, after their bear phase, they now yield the same as US equities.

But rising inflation can take time to materialise. Shifting mindsets can take longer than envisaged to change. What may well be a sustainable fillip to the equity market in the shorter term is a weakening yen because of unlimited quantitative easing. A strong currency has hit exports over the years. And because the stockmarket is full of major exporters, equities are strongly influenced by fluctuations in the currency. A declining yen would be very bullish for equities. The yen-dollar rate hovered around 77 for most of 2012. Today it is 90.

And the equity market is cheap on any number of measures. Companies have grown their earnings by 50 per cent over the last 12 years and their return on equity, a key guide to profitability, has risen from 6 per cent to 10 per cent. A strong yen has encouraged cost-cutting and production being moved to lower cost countries in Asia. Many companies also trade at below book value – the 'break-up' worth of the company's assets. By comparison, the FTSE 100 sits at around one-and-a-half times book value. Furthermore, their restructuring has left balance sheets strong, whilst they spend more on R&D than any other developed economy.

In short, these companies are now lean and mean. But the stockmarket's spring coil has remained compressed for a long time because of deflation and a strong yen. Shinzo Abe's policies could well be the catalyst to change this. Investors should take note and profit from the 'Abe Trade'. Of course, this will not be a smooth road. The Japanese establishment is conservative by nature. The BoJ knows how to put up a fight. But a landslide victory and policy so far suggest this will not be yet another false dawn.

Portfolio changes

BGFD, introduced into the Growth portfolio in December, is run by the well-respected Sarah Whitley. The trust has a good track record and gearing of around 18 per cent which, when speaking with Sarah, confirmed their optimism for the market. It has done well in the short time it has been with us.

However, it tends not to hedge the currency. I have therefore increased the Growth portfolio's exposure to Japan by introducing an ETF which hedges the yen against the GBP – namely the iShares MSCI Japan Monthly GBP Hedged ETF (IJPH). This should mean UK investors will not have any equity market gains trimmed by the extent the yen weakens against the GBP. IJPH has exposure to the largest 300 companies which should also compensate for BGFD's modest bias towards the mid-caps.

I rarely use hedged investments, believing currencies are notoriously difficult to predict as politicians and central bankers often interfere. But it is warranted here given that a weakening currency is an important ingredient to the story. This purchase has been funded by top-slicing Temple Bar Trust (TMPL), whilst standing at a premium to NAV, and City Natural Resources Trust (CYN) – both having had good runs recently.

Otherwise, there were no changes to the Income portfolio.

John Baron waives his fee for this column in lieu of donations by Investors Chronicle *to charities of his choice. As these are live portfolios, he has interests in all of the investments mentioned.*

Source: Baron J. (2013) 'Japan: a once in a lifetime opportunity?', *Investors Chronicle*, 7 February.

References

Introduction

1 Leonora Walters (2012) 'RDR: What it means for you', *Investors Chronicle*, 21 December.

2 Elaine Moore (2012) 'Fears grow over advice gap', Money section *Financial Times*, 10/11 November.

Chapter 2

1 Referred to in: James McKeigue (2011) 'Funds: the huge difference a small fee makes', *MoneyWeek*, 6 May.

2 Referred to in: Moira O'Neill (2011) 'Unique benefits of investment trusts', *Investors Chronicle*, 2 August.

Chapter 5

1 Referred to in: Alice Ross (2011) 'Understand ETF risks, investors warned', Money section, *Financial Times*, 24/25 September.

2 Referred to in: James McKeigue (2011) 'The advantages of sitting tight', *MoneyWeek*, 2 December.

3 Referred to in: Steve Lodge (2011) 'Swing towards momentum', Money section, *MoneyWeek*, 12/13 February.

Chapter 6

1 *MoneyWeek* (2013) 'Where UK stocks are heading in the long term', 15 March.

2 Elaine Moore (2011) 'FSA warns on portfolio risks', Money section, *Financial Times*, 18/19 June.

3 Referred to in: Beth Holmes (2013) 'Small fish in a big pond', February, www.cisi.org.

Chapter 7

1 Tim Bennett (2009) 'Why drip feeding won't make you rich', *MoneyWeek*, 19 June.

2 Referred to in: Alice Ross (2010) 'Market timing errors prove too costly', Money section, *Financial Times*, 20/21 November.

3 Ibid.

4 Ibid.

5 Published on 9 June 2011 in the *Financial Analysts Journal*, Vol. 67, No. 3.

6 Referred to in: Tim Bennett (2009) 'Three basic rules for investment success', *MoneyWeek*, 28 August.

7 Referred to in: Matthew Allan (2012) 'UK dividends hit record high', *Investors Chronicle*, 25 July.

Chapter 8

1 Quoted in: James Montier (2009) 'Nine rules for value investors', *Investors Chronicle*, 12 June.

Index